Please return on or before the date below.

Who Are the English?
Selected Poems 1935-81

Jack Lindsay

Smoke
STACK
BOOKS

Smokestack Books
PO Box 408, Middlesbrough TS5 6WA
e-mail: info@smokestack-books.co.uk
www.smokestack-books.co.uk

Who Are the English? Selected Poems 1935-81
Poems copyright the estate of Jack Lindsay.
Introduction copyright Anne Cranny-Francis.

ISBN 9780992740931

Smokestack Books is
represented by Inpress Ltd

Contents

Preface

In 1936 Jack Lindsay read a review in the *TLS* of Allen Hutt's *This Final Crisis*. The reviewer had dismissed the book's arguments regarding the history of Chartism on the grounds that a writer like Hutt could never really understand 'the nature of the English people' because he was a communist. Lindsay was not then a member of the Communist Party (he joined sometime around 1941), but he was incensed by the idea that the 'English people' was a mysterious and essential category of which only a few people had privileged understanding. 'Clearly,' he wrote 'we have to teach these gentlemen history as well as economics.' By way of reply he wrote a long poem, 'Who are the English?' and sent it to the magazine *Left Review*, where it was immediately published. It was subsequently issued as a pamphlet; a few weeks later it was staged as a Mass Declamation at Unity Theatre in London.

The question, 'who are the English?' was of particular importance to Jack Lindsay, since he had only recently immigrated to the UK. Jack Lindsay was born in 1900 in Melbourne, Australia. His father was the renowned – and controversial – painter Norman Lindsay. After reading Classics at the University of Queensland, Lindsay moved to Sydney, and then in 1926 to London, where he established the Fanfrolico Press and the *London Aphrodite*. Neither press nor magazine were successful; unable to afford the passage home, Lindsay retreated to the West Country, writing and publishing poetry, fiction, biography, philosophy, translations and children's stories. He never returned to Australia.

By the time he wrote 'Who Are the English?' Lindsay had published almost forty books, including translations of Aristophanes, Petronius, Sappho, Homer, Catullus and Theocritus, and the 'Prelude to Christianity' trilogy of popular historical novels, *Rome for Sale* (1934), *Caesar is Dead* (1934) and *Last Days with Cleopatra* (1935).

'Who Are the English?' marked a significant shift in Lindsay's interests, away from the Classical world and towards English history. Over the next few years he wrote two historical studies of the English Civil War, *John Bunyan* (1937) and *Sue Verney* (1937), a trilogy of historical novels about the English radical tradition, *1649: A Novel of a Year* (1938), *Lost Birthright* (1939) and *Men of '48* (written in 1939, but not published until 1948), a short popular history *England My England* (1939), and edited (with Edgell Rickword) the influential Left Book Club anthology *A Handbook of Freedom* (1939).

Publication of 'Who Are the English?' brought Lindsay into contact with leading CP writers like Rickword and Swingler, with whom he was to work closely in the pages of *Left Review, Poetry and the People* and *Our Time*. 'Who Are the English?' was consistent with the Party's attempts in the late 1930s to popularise the idea of a radical national tradition. Following the Seventh World Congress of the Comintern, when Dimitrov had argued that the success of Fascism was based in part on its ability to mobilise the Past against the Present, communists had begun looking for imaginative ways to intervene in the popular apprehension of English history.

'Who Are the English?' also marked a significant change in Lindsay's thinking about poetry. Up to this point his poetry had been influenced by his father's Dionysian aesthetic – anti-Modernist, Classical and Vitalist – publishing slim limited edition pamphlets like *Fauns and Ladies* (1923), *Spanish Main and Tavern* (1924) and *The Passionate Neatherd* (1926) and unstageable Georgian verse-plays like *Marina Faliero* (1927) and *Hereward* (1929).

Writing for a new and wider audience meant writing in a new way, in a voice that was both plainer and more rhetorical, declamatory, urgent and public, addressing the series of political crises through which he lived. During the 1930s, Lindsay's poetry was preoccupied with the struggle against European Fascism, particularly in Spain. During the Second World War, he served in the Royal Signal Corps, before being transferred to the MOI to work as a script writer for the Army Bureau of Current Affairs. He published two long verse-sequences, *Into Action: the Battle of Dieppe* (1942) and *Second Front* (1944).

By the 1950s, Lindsay was a senior figure in the Communist Party's cultural life, a crucial link with mainstream literary London and with distinguished Communist writers in Europe. His poetry was unavoidably shaped by the pressures of the Cold War – notably the civil war in Greece, the war in Korea, the Peace Movement and the events of 1956. He attended the 1948 World Congress of Intellectuals for Peace in Wroclaw, the 1949 Paris Peace Congress and the 1949 Pushkin celebrations in the Soviet Union. He visited Czechoslovakia in 1950, Poland in 1951, Romania in 1952 and 1953, and in 1954 he attended the Second Soviet Writers' Congress in Moscow. He reviewed regularly for the *Daily Worker* and was responsible for the publication in English of several writers from the 'People's Democracies'. A hostile review in the *TLS* of Lindsay's *Byzantium into Europe* (1952) concluded by calling for a purge of Communist Party members from British universities.

At the same time, Lindsay's developing ideas about culture, national tradition and democracy brought him increasingly into opposition with the Party leadership. He was on the board of Fore Publications, whose ill-fated 'Key Poets' series (including his own *Three Letters to Nikolai Tikhonov*) was denounced in the *Daily Worker* in 1950. He was also one of the founding editors of the literary magazine *Arena*, publishing European writers like Pasternak, Camus, Eluard, Tzara and Cassou in the face of severe Zhdanovite disapproval from the Party's cultural apparatus. Although other members of this 'Cultural Opposition' (notably Rickword, Swingler and the young Edward Thompson) left the Party in 1956, Lindsay remained in the Party until his death in 1990.

Lindsay continued writing poetry all his life. In 1981, his *Collected Poems* was published, running to 604 pages. When Jack Lindsay died in 1990 he had written, translated and edited over 170 books.

A note on the text

This selection is based on the texts used in Jack Lindsay's *Collected Poems* (The Cheiron Press, 1981), apart from 'Who Are the English?' which is based on the original version published in *Left Review*. For reasons of space, this selection does not include Lindsay's long verse-sequences, *Into Action: the Battle of Dieppe* (1942) and *Clue of Darkness* (1949).

Introduction

'... and the moons smelt of oranges': the poetics and politics of embodiment in Jack Lindsay's poetry

Jack Lindsay's poetry was a direct expression of values and beliefs that continued to develop over his lifetime – that we are embodied individuals, not disembodied minds; that art must appeal to the whole person, not solely to either intellect or sensation; and that politics is a lived experience, not a set of ideological principles. This understanding of the fundamental interrelationship of mind and body set Jack Lindsay's work apart from many of his peers throughout the twentieth century. It meant that his work was fundamentally misunderstood and often condemned as nostalgic romanticism by his literary peers – both members of the literary establishment and, at times, his comrades in the Communist Party of Great Britain. Both conservative and left wing contemporaries also differed from Lindsay in the way they lived their beliefs. As feminist writers were later to expose in their notion that 'the personal is political', political beliefs that are abandoned at the front door are simply a form of masquerade to convince the world of the political rectitude of the wearer. In an unpublished manuscript entitled *The Fullness of Life: The Autobiography of an Idea* Lindsay argues the same approach to political being:

> One point in common in all my phases has been the need to live wholly in accord with the dominant idea. Not to treat ideas and beliefs as a sort of luxury-product, as something to be taken out at convenient moments, brushed up, and put on display, then stowed away again till the next convenient moment. I have always tried, to the limit of my ability and understanding, to incarnate the idea, without trimming or compromise, in every aspect of my living.

Accordingly, then, for Lindsay his poetry – like all other aspects of his life and work – is inherently political. And in order for it to appeal to the embodied individual, it must interrelate bodily, sensuous appeal with conceptual (including political) understanding. As he writes in *Fullness* about the thinking behind his early book, *Dionysos: Nietzsche contra Nietzsche* (1927): 'Next, the insistence on the lived-through, the living-through; on thought-thinking not on thought-thought. This philosophy is the opposite of all those which have sought definitive systems'. The distinction between 'thought-thinking' and 'thought-thought' is that between embodied engagement and disembodied thought; between a concept of thinking that values the input of embodied being and one which believes that bodily input is 'transcended' in thought. I will briefly exemplify these underlying of principles of Lindsay's poetry, with reference to a number of poems in the volume and to Lindsay's mature analysis of his own work in *Fullness*. Lindsay notes that poetry was his earliest passion:

> Only in poetry I felt the conflict [between permanence and change] reconciled and the courage to confront a divided world: a triumphant kinship with all who had ever sung or loved in the remotest gulfs of time, and with all who would yet sing or love; and yet the irremediable pathos of the precarious isolation of the singer or lover, his face immediately blurred in the black wind. So, till near the end of my teens, I cannot remember ever thinking about what my career was going to be. I lived in the moment of absorption by poetry, which dominated my studies.

The description of the poet/lover with his face already blurred by the winds of time incorporates the combination of bodily presence and conceptual understanding/vision that characterizes much of Lindsay's writing. Laurence Coupe quotes Lindsay from his essay, 'The Modern Consciousness', first published in 1928 in the *London Aphrodite*: 'I… take as my criterion the concrete universal, the human dynamic.' This notion of the 'concrete universal' might seem a contradiction for those whose notion of a universal is an abstracted essence and fundamentally metaphysical. For Lindsay, however, this abstraction was deeply problematic as it denied the everyday experience of being. Coupe notes that in the same essay Lindsay praised Kant 'for attempting to reconcile mind and matter, idea and world, and in effect destroying all metaphysics'. Lindsay's poetry works to the same end, bringing together mind and matter, idea and world. Consider, for example, these lines from 'On Guard for Spain':

> After the February elections
> the people sang in the streets of work.
> The echoes of time were notes of guitars
> and the moons smelt of oranges
> amid the jasmine-stars.

Here the Spanish people's sense of political and social justice is expressed in images of bodily engagement (singing in the streets), the senses (time/music, moons/oranges, jasmine/stars) and synaesthesia (visual/olfactory; moon/orange). At the same time, the images chosen – singing, guitars, oranges – evoke the cultural imaginary and embodied experience of Spain for a British audience. The political environment of joy and hope, which precedes the fascist takeover, is thereby rendered as a complex of bodily experience – sensory, embodied, conceptual; the people embody the joyful experience of political equity, as does the audience of the Declamation.

Lindsay's poem to Tristan Tzara, 'Paris Midnight' opens with a stanza that shows the same interweaving of political commentary and embodied engagement:

> Tristan you first discovered
> under bibles, advertisement-hoardings, and metaphysics
> that Chaos was not a primordial condition
> but an involuntary invention
> of bourgeois cuttlefish
> exuding darkness to confuse the issue
> and find themselves at home.

Tzara learns/reveals that religion, modern consumerism and idealist philosophy offer no answers but are used by bourgeois capitalism to conceal the reality of its social practice and organization, and that the apologists of capitalism (bourgeois cuttlefish) invent notions of pre-capitalist chaos and disorder in order to justify their own regulatory and disciplinary practices. The mixture of material references – bibles, hoardings, cuttlefish – with the meanings they signify – religion, capitalism, obfuscation – exemplifies the same interrelationship of everyday embodied experience and thinking. Again, this is 'thought-thinking' not 'thought-thought' with Tzara's embodied experience represented by these concrete references to the everyday, while the meanings they signify are revealed as critical to his poetic and political practice.

The same dialectic is evident in a late poem Lindsay wrote to his estranged father, Norman Lindsay 'in your hermitage/ of cold and scornful stone,/ of tranquil and ruthless light'. Their relationship had a very turbulent history but ended in silence and the poem ends with this heart-breaking request:

> Turn for a moment I say
> turn from your obdurate place
> in that clarity of stone,
> that terrible folly of light,
> turn for a moment this way
> your abstracted face.

In the poem Norman is not simply a distant patriarchal non/presence but palpably there, situated in his Blue Mountains (west of Sydney) home, amid the granite outcrops of that region and under the clear, strong light of Australia. For Jack, this physical location reflects the qualities in his father that keep them apart – Norman's obdurate certainty about the correctness of his own views, which he maintains with absolute clarity and without mercy. This representation of Norman as 'abstracted' is a final acknowledgment (and condemnation) of his father's rejection of the everyday material world and retreat into an idealist fantasy that enabled him to cut himself off from those who did not agree with or humour him.

To Jack abstraction signified the removed, intellectualized, transcendent consciousness that enables individuals to act without empathy and without mercy. Describing in *Fullness* their joint (father/son) aims for Fanfrolico Press in London, he wrote: ' …we were in fact strongly patriotic, seeing Europe as culturally exhausted, going down into a swamp of primitivism, a desert of abstraction' and, even more urgently, he wrote of their joint artistic project: 'The sensuous image was coming to life, we believed, in the night of abstraction, the death of man'. Abstraction is here equated with the end of all they understand as humanity. Also, in his early book, *William Blake: Creative Will and the Poetic Image* (1927) Lindsay wrote that Blake identified two conditions that afflict the human soul: 'The first is all that tends to harden, to parch, to lose vital contact with life and set up an intellectual or moral abstraction in place of the living image'. The abstraction that he grieves in Norman at the end of his life is not only his personal indifference, but also the loss of that early passion to create a richer understanding of life that involved the interrelation of mind and body (the living image). As Jack explains in *Fullness,* he saw abstraction as the philosophical move or stance that enabled ideologically driven systems such as fascism and capitalism to flourish, and to generate the repression and alienation of individuals that characterize them. Norman was totally opposed to direct political action and had no sympathy for Jack's political views, which was one reason (among many) for their estrangement. All of this – Norman's withdrawal from Jack's life (again), his refusal to engage with the world around him, his tacit support for deeply conservative politics – is compressed into that one image of Norman, head averted, gazing into the distance.

Related to this understanding of individual consciousness as fundamentally embodied (not abstracted from the everyday material world) is the need to write of and for the whole person. An interesting context for this is Lindsay's response to D.H. Lawrence's work, which he disliked for what he called its 'sex mysticism'. In his essay, 'The Modern Consciousness' published in the journal, *London Aphrodite* (1928) he described Lawrence as 'the opposed twin of Eliot and Lewis', noting: 'He wants the loss of identity, not its hellenised godhead. He wants to ooze back into the mud, masochistically surrendering to the brutal embrace of death, not to shape Praxitelean statues from his poised delight.' Though Lindsay later acknowledged that over time he came to appreciate Lawrence's understanding of 'the nature of alienation and of the cash-nexus', his instinctive response is to reject what he saw in Lawrence's work as the fetishization of the sexual, at the expense of an integrated (embodied) being. The value of this contrast is simply to clarify that Lindsay was not arguing for a reversal of the mind/body dichotomy (valuing the body), but for its replacement with a fully integrated understanding of being or consciousness. This can be seen in the opening of Lindsay's poem, 'To Ann' written for his partner, Ann Davies (also known as Ann Lindsay):

When lovers meet

at deep noon or midnight
the torrent of history
pours roaring on them

This image of lovers meeting combines the bodily (sensory) and the intellectual or cerebral. The lovers meet and the world contracts to a roaring cataract of their own senses, thoughts, emotions, in which they encounter only each other. Their perception of each other is sensory – like our visual discernment of day and night, our hearing of a waterfall, our feeling of its spray – and intellectual – the history of love and lovers; of the meetings of like souls. Mind and body are evoked in the same images that are themselves both material (everyday world of noon and midnight, the torrent) and conceptual (lovers, history). For Lindsay this attempt to achieve 'fullness' or integration or 'unity' is the aim of life, so a later stanza declares the lovers' responsibility to contribute to their world:

When lovers meet
secure in the stormwind
Life hands them all things:
'Redeem, transform.'

In other words, the responsibility of lovers is not simply to retire from the world into their own safe space, but to use their joint energy to make a better world. Lindsay goes on to specify that this will be a communist future, which for him meant a world without class or alienation or injustice.

> When lovers meet
> nothing is lost:
> the communist future
> once grasped in our hands

This is not the kind of sentiment that many would expect in a love poem, but it is crucial for Lindsay for whom love cannot be abstracted away from our living in the world, which in turn is where our responsibility lies. The meeting of lovers, then, is sensory and emotional, intellectual, cultural, social and political.

In a very different poem, 'Where Are We Hopelessly Wrong?' (1953) Lindsay reflects on the experience of debating social problems and how to solve them in Marx House, London. He begins by evoking the bodily experience of such a meeting; sitting in a hot, humid, dusty room trying to keep awake as people debate around him/us:

> The plumes of heat are sprinkling dust
> Our faces lift their furtive lids
> close down again and bodies creak
> upon the chairs of polyp growth.

We start to understand and like plants growing towards the sun, our thoughts rise and our bodies straighten, until fear strikes:

> Higher we rise on tenuous stakes
> of comprehension till we rub
> green-haloed heads along the ceiling
> then sink upon a spike of fear

And we see our own inadequacies and fears reflected in the arguments of our opponents:

> and look again on our own faces
> from unsuspected mirrors set
> by enemies in midst of words
> to turn them on more complex axes

Yet the world we have now and the world we want to create is more than this endless debate:

> and yet the world is never further
> than the revolving windows blown
> by the dark breath of weathercocks
> into the dawn of all the peoples

Lindsay's frustration with the Communist Party meetings and their endless discussion is articulated in a poem that embodies his feeling; we sense not only his intellectual exasperation at the failure of the political argument, but also his bodily presence in that room – and we know that, for him, the two are intimately related. And this, after all, is a key element of his political argument: that we cannot abstract people from their everyday lives and expect to relate to them, to be able to work with them, or to create a viable new society.

For Lindsay, as noted earlier, politics is a lived experience, not just a set of ideas or dogma. The poems discussed above argue this point, as Lindsay represents the life and work of Tristan Tzara, his embodied experience of political argument in the Communist Party of Great Britain and his love for Ann. In each case the politics of a person, situation or a relationship is expressed as fundamental to their being and experience. In his verse declamation, 'Who Are the English?' (1936) we find the same understanding of politics as arising out of, and also as forming, the lived experience of the individual. In this long, dramatized poem Lindsay deconstructs mainstream history, 'the definition of the ruling class' and in its place presents a detailed account of the working-class leaders and movements that have shaped the English character and its people – John Ball, Jack Cade, Wycliffe, the Lollards, Anabaptists, Levellers, Chartists and Socialists, among many others.

Early in the poem Lindsay quotes the Lollard priest, John Ball who played a key role in the Peasants' Revolt of 1381:

> When Adam delved and Eve span,
> who was then the gentleman?
> You are not English, peasant.
> your ruling class has said it.

Sung by the women, Ball's famous lines reflect the question of Lindsay's title and alert the listener/reader to the historical depth of his inquiry. This is not just about the twentieth-century but includes all the centuries of living and working together that have formed the character of the English people. The denial of Englishness to the peasantry (Man's voice) refers to the formal exclusion of the workers from both the political process and the historical narrative. The declamation then goes on to refute this ruling class claim, showing the role workers have played throughout history and that they continue to play with their vision of a socialist republic, which is their England. Male and female voices, chorus and semi-chorus, literally articulate the involvement of all as individuals, classes and a nation in this history, while the movements that Lindsay specifies for speakers signify, in a direct way, that this is an embodied engagement, not simply a clash of ideologies.

In the final pages of *Fullness* Lindsay writes:

> The artist, the poet, the musician, who matters, is he who catches and defines this moment of freedom, of *Aufhebung* (transcendence), in the concrete here-and-now. Utopian ideas and aspirations to definite goals in the future may well play a part in his synthesis; indeed in some degree or other they cannot fail to be present; but the essential thing, the aesthetic core, lies in the concrete apprehension of the living moment as one of freedom, of the three freedoms defined by Marx.

Lindsay's genius was in his specific location of the person, idea or practice within the concrete reality of the everyday. That reality includes both the history that has formed it and the aspirations and dreams of those who live it, all of which is compressed into what he goes on to describe as '*the concrete humanity of the particular moment*'. This description might be read as Lindsay's manifesto for his own writing and as a tribute to the richness and value of the poetry he left for us.

Anne Cranny-Francis
University of Technology, Sydney, Australia
August 2014

References

Coupe, Lawrence. (1984) 'Jack Lindsay: From the Aphrodite to Arena' in R. Mackie (ed), *Jack Lindsay: The Thirties and Forties*

Lindsay, Jack and P.R. Stephensen. (1928-1912) *The London Aphrodite*. London: Fanfrolico Press.

Lindsay, Jack. (1927) *William Blake: Creative Will and the Poetic Image*. London: Fanfrolico Press.

Lindsay, Jack. (1981) *Collected Poems*. Lake Forest, Ill.: Chiron Press.

Lindsay, Jack. (n.d.) *Dionysos: Nietzsche Contra Nietzsche, an essay in lyrical philosophy*. London: Fanfrolico Press.

Lindsay, Jack. (n.d.) *The Fullness of Life: The Autobiography of An Idea*, unpublished manuscript.

Mackie, Robert, ed. (1984) *Jack Lindsay: The Thirties and Forties*. London: University of London, Institute of Commonwealth Studies, Australian Studies Centre.

First Fears and Misapprehensions

Will you take me, workers? will you take me as one
of yourselves? I have stripped time's rags and stand naked.
I have thrown away the past, all that I've wastefully done;
that's ended now, I have no reason to shun
your eyes. I offer my hand. Will you take it?
I had sheltered early-years yet darkly threaded
by the child's suffering when parents quarrel and break.
But I was not thrown out in the world. I was fed
though with sickening food. I was fed. I'd a bed though I lay awake.

I have wandered far, hiding from faces of shame,
though I did not know the truth. Now I wholly know it.
I have been bitten through the cord of the strangled dream
between the bull-bellow and the siren-scream,
and only in manhood now do I find the worth of the poet.
Manhood is yours, you workers. Yours alone.
You are life's fine ceaseless pattern mocking despair.
I thought you'd trample the fields that beauty has sown –
you that are earth and harvest, quick with the shapes of the air.

I have learned what hunger is. I have tightened my belt.
and gone out to walk on the beach that the seagulls owned.
I have lived for weeks on a few potatoes, and felt
the rats crawl on me from slums of sleep, and smelt
the ghosts of fear that out of blood-darkness moaned.
I have shivered in the cold, having no coal or wood.
I have walked with chilblains on the spikes of frost,
and in the appalled disrelish of the thwarted blood
have known my flesh a desert where a child was born.

I have gone further now. I have come out beyond
in the comradeship accepting the world's greatest task.
I know what holds stars in the sky, I know what strikes out of the ground
the flower-sparks of the spring, I have touched the bond.
Only you can help me, only your aid I ask,
and you have given it since the fount was unsealed
and waters sparkled to wash the grime of my pains.
The world's outrage on my remembering flesh was healed.
Workers, I too have nothing to lose but my chains.

Summering Song

I lay and listened to the long lisping
of summer in wheat and slept beneath warm
a soft sly surge of whispering wheat-ears
rustling with blitheness ripe across birdlull
a sea of summer surfed on the stripes
lushtangle of hedge and the hawkweed clusters
cut in serenity high on the sky-banks
I slumbered fast and summer flowed over
in a weaving of waves the slow rumour of wheat
till golden I glimpsed the green ripples gossiping
sealed on the sky and spicily blown
thistle-beards twisted in bloom of the blue

Over all England entered this bright breeze
between the birdsongs blurred in the soughing
of summer I drowsed and I drowned underneath
till came two visions clear out of vastness
the past and the future both pierced in a fashion
both knotted in hands that held in their keeping
the full land furrowed and flailed with lean labour

The peasants rising with rage and patience
against enclosures of ancient earths
with mattock and spade shaggily mustering
wrenched up the fences and walls around fallow
unfastening fields with a faith in unity:
they ran and they laughed with a leap into rapture
songs of blest islands invoked in a sweat
bristling with wealth and blazing westward
with fountains of wine in a flame of red wind
with ample apples and pancake palaces
preciously dyed for a promised discovery

Filling the ditches they drudged with a fury
and night came down in a fever of dreams
they lay in a labyrinth with love's own laughter
and star-blossoms crackled as blue as chickory:
the nightjar thudding in thickets of nuts
cried doom on devils: and lovers with litanies
moaned in high lofts or meadows of lustre
cradled in hay: the crowds in christ's hunger
hurried for eden happily ensigned
and the dawn swung up with a snarl of trumpets
cried doom on devils: the yaffle went yiking:
on water-meadows with wings downpointed
the tidy redshank dropped with a trill:
sweet-apples rifted the russet shadows:
the deer sprang dappled on silver streams
all for loose life and the lap of the loving
the liberty-leap and the loyal of laughter

I speak with a song
for peasant-camps captained by Kett or by Pouch
an instant fronting the fate of England
a single swathe set for the scything
the songs of the promise: they sowed on their pathway
bullvoice of noon with braggart nostrils
the hour of the heron in moonstruck musing
a bubble-sweetness burst with the starwort
glistening in grasses and gingerly grappling
with hooks of its leaves that hoist to the light
burst in a breathing of waspish winds
smasht by the soldiers of wary sheriffs
gasping in ditchdeaths on gallows-elms
gagged and gaping for carrion-crows

The hidden barriers broke their high hopes
the foe that they smelt but failed still to see
the foulfiends of money feeding on manhood
beelzebubs coiling in bills of credit:
they fell on failure my friends and their flags
these men who woke to march on a world
with an axe and a song in the arch of the spring
the women wading weeping in waters
breast-high to drive at the bonds of the dykes
and children hacking at the hedge-cruelties
that cut us apart in a private confusion:
they failed and they fell and the king's forces
trod flat their faces in fields forgotten
back to earth's blessing with blocks and boulders

Peasants claiming your birthright commons
and losing England in longpast centuries
O larkpulse of morning lovely and mettlesome
you are still England
titmouse with long tail laired in the thornbush
the story's not ended or England ended
the sentry of marshland the redshank mutters:
the springmarch is drumming and the sap of danger:
We are still England

The peasants' passion climbs in the coverts
and deepens the tarn of troubled darkness:
the dreams of the people plead with the dead
and the devils fear in the damned faces
of England's evil in city-streets
O let me live through the hell-harrowing
to view the murdered victorious march
as now they march in the noon of these murmurs
singing with standards of summer-sweetness
through England cleared into equal commons
and barriers broken
O peasant prophets
of fenceless plenty risen to ring me
lying here listening to whispering wheat-ears
on earth's bared bosom.

Who Are the English?

Who are the English,
according to the definition
of the ruling class?
All you that went forth,
lured by great sounding names
which glittered like bubbles of crystal in your eyes
till they burst and you burst with them, shot to shreds,
from one end of the shuddering earth to the other end,
shot that the merchants pockets might clink and bulge,
shot that hoardings of imperial size
might fill each blank space of the motor roads
with pink whore-faces beckoning the bankrupt to buy –
you are the English
your ruling class has said it
you are the English,
keep then the recompense of a sounding name, for you have
    nothing else.

Or you, the ragged thief, fruit of the press gang, gallowsbird,
flogged to a scarlet-breasted musketeer,
you, too, splintered your bones to build an Empire;
and now that names are lost in the desolation of moons,
snow drifting on the war gnawed litter of history,
the dump of bones, you starveling, accept your share
with those whom the great sounding names or greed
drew with drum flams to death in distant places,
while Flanders mud flakes off the latest dump,
you are the English
your ruling class has said it.

And shuffle along you toilers on whose cowed faces
the heels of your betters have left bleeding badges
as proof of your allegiance. Shuffle along,
all you thrifty cotters saved from brotherhood by Wesley.
all you farmhands sweated out of thought,
all you slum denizens humbly paying pence
to keep a Bishop in Christian poverty,
all you shophands beaten over the brain
till you can only answer, 'O let's go to the pictures,'
all you that lick the hand providing dope,
you readers of the national newspapers
absorbing fascism and astrology
with your list of winners and hire-payment systems,
you, you, you are the English
your ruling class has said it.
Keep then the recompense of a sounding name, for you have
    nothing else.

I call instead on those who are not the English
according to the definition of the ruling class.
We'll step back first six hundred years or seven
and call up the peasants hoarsely talking under the wind,
their cattle stolen by the king's purveyors,
their wives deceived by whining hedge-priests,
Peasants leaving your wattled huts to haunt
the crooked dreams of Henry with your scythes,
unrolling a long scroll you couldn't read
though you knew the word it held, not England,
but Justice – come, you peasants with hoof smashed faces,
speak from the rotting wounds of your mouths, we'll
    understand
prompting you with our anger.

I talked with John Ball, I was out with Jack Cade
I listened to Wicliffe, I was burnt as a Lollard.
Come with us peasants, waking from fumes of charcoal,
into the wintry dawn, while the cattle stamp,
leap from your strawbed, leave the blowsy alewife,
someone has called, and you have taken your fork,
against the thundering cataphract of power.
When Adam delved and Eve span,
who was then the gentleman?
You are not English, peasant.
your ruling class has said it.
Come with us, then, for our love and our indignation
conjure you out of the dung, and we'll avenge you.
Come with us peasant, we've the wind in our teeth
we're out in the night, hunting, hunting but not to trample
the crops of the poor, we have another quarry.
Rise up, peasants, listening to the many voices,
fall in behind us, you are not English, comrades.

I call on those who left the little farms
and left the common lands at Parliament's voice
to chase the grave and comely henpecked king.
I call on Cromwell's Ironsides and the men
who listened to the many voices blown, distracted,
birdcries out of the thicket of blood-darkness,
and answered awry, glamoured by dark phrases,
the slaughtered Lamb, the flayed carcass of their lives,
the unremitting call to follow truth,
to follow a bond denying their present slavery,
broken by harsh echoes from the unploughed thicket.
Come, you Anabaptists and you Levellers,
come, you Muggletonians, all you Bedlamites,
fall in behind us, you are not English, comrades.

Come, you Luddites, come you men of the Charter,
singing your songs of defiance on the blackened hills,
invoking the storm, the whirlwind, being surer now,
deciphering at last the certain earth behind
the many voices confusing the moonstruck mind.
Come from the mines and the looms, come from the
    ploughlands,
from the minds and the looms,
come and tramp the streets of Birmingham and London,
the dragoon are waiting to spit your skulls, my comrades,
for you are not English, you angry millions, you workers,
your voice snarls in the clang of the flaring foundry,
your voice rips louder than the raven caws at morning,
you are speaking out and were not meant to speak,
you are waking, comrades,
you are not English now,
your ruling class has said it.
You spoke at Glasgow and the Clyde when terrorism
was jailing all men in the roaring jail of war;
you will speak louder yet.
It came, the first full throated shout of your purpose
in 1926, in the General Strike.
Pickets against police, the new order against the old,
Councils of Action against the State of the thieves.
There was laughter despite hunger, life blossomed with
    meaning
amid the red rust and the deserts of slag,
and brotherhood woke with new clearness from the act of
    your union.
You were defeated by your wavering leaders,
the purpose was driven down, to breed greater strength in
    your depths.

Stand out one of the men who were not English,
come, William Morris,
you that preached revolt to the workers and said
of the men who died for us in the Commune of Paris:
We honour them as the foundation-stone
of the new world that is to be.
You that cried out after Bloody Sunday.
Not one, not one, nor thousands must they slay,
but one and all if they would dusk the day!
And stand out you the unknown weaver,
who wrote in the *Poor Man's Guardian* of 1832,
before Marx has shown us how the thefts were made:
the profit is that which is retained and never paid back,
there is no common interest
between working men and profit makers.

You were not English, we are not English either –
though we have these trees plumed upon the sunset
and turned back to the area rails our prison bars;
though we have followed the plough like a hungry rook
with love for the brown soil slicing fatly away,
to haunt in the end the dingy rain of the street
where a prosperous splith of warming music
trickled through drawn blinds on our beggar senses;
though we have crept into the daisy light of the dew
to wake once more in the dripping tenements;
though we have plucked hazelnuts in the lane of autumn,
making faces at the squirrel, to kiss between laughters,
that was not our land, we were trespassers,
the field of toil was our allotted life,
beyond it we might not stir though blossom scents
left tender trails leading to the heart of summer;
though we have loved this earth where our seat and our tears
drained through the thankless centuries, though we lay
long nights of agony digging our fingers deep
in the wet earth, yet the bailiffs evicted us,
it was all taken away, England was taken,
what little of it was ours in desperate toil
was taken, and the desperate toil remained

and lanes of dank gloom where the echo of midnight falls
a late wayfarer stumbling, leaving nothing behind
except the gaslight coughing and the crying child,
milk turned sour in the thunder hour awaiting,
queues at the Labour Exchange while the radio squeals
in the shop nearby, and nothing remains, nothing
except the mad faces forming from the damp stains on the plaster,
the scabs of sickness and the jagged edge
of tins in the bucket, and the knock on the door,
and the child crying and the bug heats, hunger, hunger,
and the child crying
and the radio-message through crevices of the dark silence
Workers of the World...
Listen, hold up your head, it wasn't the rat
whisking under the coal scuttle, it wasn't the lodger
stealing back scared from the woman under the bridge.
In this hour even the flower lips speak. It is
the augural moment declared by frenetic guesses,
come clear at last. The moon slit whispers, the rafter
creaks to a new pulse stirring, the bough of silence
cracks with a quick decision, men softly creeping
through forests of hardship to surprise the drunken castle.
Lift up your head,
listen, you Rhondda miners, you Durham miners,
the radio voice is seeping through the barriers,
Workers of the World...
They are awake at Bleanleachan, men are stirring,
reaching out their hands, the moon sets in the coal tip,
the fans of the air shaft whirr like a giant breathing.
Come, changelings of poverty, cheated of the earth,
Albion or Land of Brut or Avalon,
Coal-ghetto that was once the Isle of Apples,
call it what you will, there must be in it
Socialist Republic.
England, my England –
the words are clear
Workers of the World, unite!
The voice comes pealing through the trumpet of the night,
You have nothing to lose but your chains!

The sunlight breaks
like waves on a shingly beach, sweeping the mountains
with more than the sough of pines.
This morning is of men as well as light
its unity is born from the sweat of mingled toil,
it springs from the earth of action,
its is ours and England. We who made it, we are making
another England, and the loyalty learned
in mine and factory begets our truth,
this compact linking is to past and future.
The workers take the world that they have made!
unseal the horns of plenty, join once more
the severed ends of work and play; and if the thieves
challenge our coming, we have learned the might
of sledged falling, the turbines fury, the craft
of dynamos winding energy from the elements.
In vain they turn their guns and poison gas
on those for whom electricity rears its unseen fortress,
the sun drops shrapnel of light upon their ranks
but feeds our renewed bodies; the womb of earth
cries for our seed. No others have the thews
to make this earth this England, breed to her desire.
The disinherited are restored, our mother,
England, our England,
England, our own.

Warning of the End

'Shock-troops disobeyed their officers dismounted, and joined the mob'
News report of events in Madrid on 17 February 1936.

Do you think that politicians and bankers do more than assume,
for the press-photographers, a face of bleared compassion
when people starve? do they hear the voice of doom
when bugs devour the slum-walls but do not lower rents?

Do you think the bourgeois turn their heads
if the hoof of famine stamps out a Chinese village?
(The Japanese have the situation in hand, eliminating the Reds.)
The bourgeois suffering comes in another fashion.

A tumbling market may disturb their pillage,
but is not serious; for they can always recoup
their losses elsewhere, pushing the workers down.
Only one matter gives them tears to shed,
only one bellykick makes their spirits droop.

That is when the shock-troops, that is when the cossacks,
sent to batter a crowd and back them dumb,
hear the voices Brother, the thundering voices Brother,
and answer We are Brothers, and laugh Brothers we come!

Looking at a Map of Spain on the Devon Coast

August, 1937

The waves that break and rumble on the sands
gleaming outside my window, break on Spain.
Southward I look and only the quick waves stretch
between my eyes and ravaged Santander moaning
with many winds of death, great blackening blasts
of devastation and little alley-whispers
where forgotten children die.

The map of Spain
bleeds under my fingers, cracked with rivers
of unceasing tears, and scraped with desolation,
and volleyed with these moaning winds of death.
Aragon I touch, Castilla, and Asturias.

The printed words black on the small white page
waver like mountains on the expanse of day.
They ring me round, sierras of history
Granite above time's stream with human meanings
that make the stars a tinsel and the thundering
waves on the rattled beach a trivial echo
of their tremendous wars.
I lean towards Spain over the thundering waters.

The brittle mask has broken, the money-mask
that hid the jackal-jaws, the mask of fear
that twisted the tender face of love; and eyes
now look on naked eyes. The map of Spain
seethes with the truth of things, no longer closed
in greed's geography, an abstract space
of imports, exports, capitalist statistics,
the jargon record of a tyrannous bargain.
The scroll of injustice, the sheet of paper is torn,
and behind the demolished surface of the lie
the Spanish people are seen with resolute faces.
They break the dark grilles
on custom's stuccoed wall
and come into the open.

In the city-square the rags of bodies lie
like refuse after death's careless fiesta.
Sandbags are plied across
the tramlines of routine.
A bullet has gone through the townhall clock,
the hands of official time are stopped.
New clocks for the Spanish people:
new springs and cogwheels for the Time of Freedom.
The garrotting machines are snatched
out of the chests of old darkness
and strung between lamp-posts and balcony
in the streets of sunlight in Barcelona.
My friend is holding the cartridge-belt, the gun
is trained on the corner, the turn in the dark street,
round which the Fascists will come.
The noticeboard of the People's University
is nailed above the church's door of stone
over the face of the Virgin in the shrine.
New clocks for the Spanish people:
New springs and cogwheels for the Time for Freedom.

These images slip through the mesh. They flush
the superficial map with hints
of what the tumult means.
You girl in overalls with young breasts of pride
bearing the great banner down the street,
your pulse accords with the day's terrific cymbals.
You militiaman leaning
beside the soup-cauldrons on the ridge of stones
and bushes flickering with heat, your hands
speak of the sickle and hammer, and the rifle
you hold in such a way
breaks to a cornsheaf in your dreaming hour
deep-rooted in Spanish earth, because you love
that girl with flower-eyes and breasts of milk
lifted with promise on the day of work
like olive-trees tousled silver under the wind.

The old man choking among the thistles
by the peaked windmill with the lattice-wings
has spoken a curse. The child blindly crying
down lanes of terror in the endless night
of bursting faces, and the mother riddled
with rape on the dungheap, and the friend
who smiled at you yesterday
now crucified on the garden-wall,
litter these names. Oh, watch the map of Spain
and you can see the sodden earth of pain,
the least blood-trickle on the broken face,
and hear the clutter of the trucks that bring
the Moorish firing-squad along the village street,
and through the frantic storm of shattering guns
the child's small wail. You hear it in your heart.
louder than all the roaring. An accusation
that shall be answered.

And louder too than all the hell of war
clanging over the tiles or the hilltops hoarse
with raiding planes, there sounds the pulse of work,
the hum of factories in communal day.
The girl with the cap of liberty at the loom
weaves the fate of Spain,
the web of brotherhood on the wrap of courage.
The factory windows crimson with the sunset
flash signals to the fields of toil;
the slow echelon of sickles
advance upon the wheat. Now in the battle
the Spanish workers ride
the horses of the year, wild mountain-horses
tamed to draw the plough of man.
Hear the confederate engines throb
the belts whirr and the hammers of power leap thudding,
to bring about at last the generous hour
when man and nature mate in plenty's bed.

Oh, Map of Spain creviced with countless graves,
even now, even now, the storm of murder comes.
The burning face of day is blind with tears.
I stand at the atlantic edge and look
southwards and raise my hand to Spain. Salute.

Christmas Eve 1937

The absent talk tonight within our hearts.
The lost ones, the forsaken, the sick and jailed
behind the bars of torture play their parts
without one word
of love to warm them: evil has prevailed
in that dark place where living they're interred.

O Spain is scarred with graves, we know it well.
Splashing the acids of quick death, there screams
into the night of man the fascist shell –
O night of Spain,
we too have heard it grinding through our dreams,
the bird of evil with scabbed claws of pain.

In Spain and China burns this Christmas Eve
with smoke of blood and vats of murderous gold
O poor ones grooved with tears, we hear you grieve:
this night is thick
with voices of your agonies untold,
you lost ones, you forsaken torn and sick.

Thaelmann is cragg'd against the sunsethour.
He coughs and listens to enormous death,
he hears the jailertread, he clasps the power
that sets men free
though he is chained alone: ah, hold your breath,
listen with Thaelmann, heart of history.

Tom Mooney sits and looks through prison bars
upon his lonely silence, sharing thus
the vigorous night that sweats with ceaseless stars,
our night of pain.
Tom Mooney fights this battle leading us
and steadily speaks in China, speaks in Spain.

In Trinidad now Uriah Butler stands
gripping the bars and Prestes in Brazil,
Mick Kane in England lifts his hidden hands,
and somewhere near,
as through the night the burning voices spill,
Chandler and Smith and Carney strain to hear.

The countless German cells, Italian cells
the fascist cells of Europe O everywhere
the pale eyes open upon dingy hells,
the webs of Spain,
the stain, the trickling hour of dull despair,
the bodies crumbling, and the voice again.

The voice goes on and on this Christmas night
as any other night and Thaelmann hears,
they hear it all, and they forget their plight,
they grip the bars,
they stare through stone of agonies and fears,
and see the swinging and unceasing stars.

And we too pause, I said. The shadows creep,
the weak light bubbles, empty is the glass,
and as we lean upon the bar of sleep,
we hear them all,
we see their figures into anguish pass,
we hear and answer their unfaltering call.

On Guard for Spain

What you shall hear is the tale of the Spanish people.
It is also your own life.
On guard, we cry!
It is the pattern of the world to-day...

I speak for the Spanish people,
I speak for the Spanish people to the workers of the world.
Men and women, come out of the numbered cells
of harsh privation, mockingly called your homes,
break through the deadening screen with your clenched fists,
unrope the bells that jangle in the steeple of the sky,
make the least gap of silence in the wall of day
and you will hear the guns in Spain.

Face here the map of your own fate, and say:
This suffering shall not be in vain.

Thus we plead with you our need.
Cannot you hear the guns in Spain?

Have you ever come out of the tangled undergrowth
into the clearing of history?
Then you have lived in Spain,
Spain of these years of pang and aspiration,
Spain the arena where a weaponless man
takes the charge of a bull of havoc,
Spain where the workers, going to battle,
go as to a fiesta,
Spain.
Salute to Spain!

After the February elections
the people sang in the streets of work.
The echoes of time were notes of guitars
and the moons smelt of oranges
amid the jasmine-stars.
Bodies that had been jailed by fear
turned to the slopes of light once more.

The sun tied ribbons in all the trees
when we led the prisoners out of the jails,
thousands of comrades came singing out
while the waves of the sea clicked castanets
from shore to dancing shore.
The locks of the prisons of poverty
were broken by the manners of unity,
and brushing the cobwebs of old night away
we came out into the factories of day.

We cried, and cried again:
On guard, people of Spain.
Franco the Butcher lurks in the Canary Islands.
Queipo de Llano in Seville mutters threats in his drunken sleep.
Batet sneers in Barcelona.
Sanjurjo waits in Lisbon for the gong of murder to sound.
Mola, masked with a grin, chats with death at Burgos.
On guard, people of Spain!

Gil Robles whispers in the jungle of darkness.
There is a chinkle of bribes, a smell of powder
in draped sacristies, and bombs beside the pyx.
The crucifix is held up by a stack of rifles.
The muddy light drowning in cathedral-aisles
favours conspirators, or their leathery faces sweat
where Juan March and bankers have a word
behind the frosted windowpane of importance,
their heads scarfed with cigar-smoke
as they smile and bend closer.

Remember, Spanish people,
the humble marchers shot down out of side-streets,
the shattered men splashed on the shattered walls of the Asturias,
the cobbles slippery with blood,
the girl screaming in the midnight of her rape,
the scythe of machine-gun volleys,
women and children mown down on red earth,
the cells of torture,
the long night of starvation,
the thugs of the Falange
sniping from taxis, hiding
round corners of the night.
Remember what was suffered in 1934.

Cry out, and cry again,
On guard, people of Spain!
But amid the guitars of laughter,
amid the orange-suns
in Liberty's newly-opened orchard,
a light of plenty
shining its promise into the crannies of slums,
and children playing
amid the carnation-glow
of the shadows of Granada,
who was there to hearken?

Why should they take our hope away?
Surely no cloud of greed can tarnish our bright day.
In spring we shall dance on the terraces by the sea,
our sweat shall make the summer gold with corn,
autumn shall ooze from the olive-presses,
and we shall pluck from our flesh sharp winter's thorn.

Then came the blow
A mailed fist of thunder struck down that sun of hope,
and in the deliberate darkness the murderers moved.
Out of the barracks of conspiracy
were led the hoodwinked soldiers.
Gold was silently spilt
to grease the wheels of counter-revolution.
Those dumps of reaction, the arsenal churches,
bared their armouries of oppression.
The fascist monster, slimed from the night,
roared out over Spain.

On guard, Spain, on guard!

Now was the testing time of the people,
now with the terrible trumpets of the dawn
crying out over the grey-green olive-slopes
that ran down to the shimmering sea,
crying out over the plains of peasant toil,
crying out over sierras of buffeted limestone,
crying out over Madrid and Barcelona,
the moment of choice appeared.
Seize it, Spanish people,
or lose it for evermore.

Are they right, the fascists,
calling the people swine,
mud to be trodden, mud that has no purpose
except to breed
the flowers of leisure for the few?

The people answered.
That dawn of crystal suddenness,
that lightning of choice,
shuddered across Spain
from the rosy heights of the Pyrenees
to the wide grey combers of the Atlantic,
from the striped valleys of Andalusia
to the tumbled crags of the Asturias.

Through hammerclang we heard it,
through clatters of looms, through chip of the machines,
down in the burning darkness of the mines,
on the red plains of dust,
along the sheeptracks on the heights of loneliness,
among the rocks of heat,
along the tinkling waterways,
where we were threshing corn in the cracked barn,
standing up in the dry shadow of the corktrees,
digging beside the silver shoals of olive-leaves,
coming off work at the junction,
wiping our oiled hands with some cotton-waste –
all over Spain we heard it.

We came from field and town, from clay-huts on the hills
and tenements of dirt. We poured out on the Ramblas,
asking for news, pulling the railings up.
Shots pitted the morning-hush.
We sought the hearts of that alarm, tracking
the spoor of danger. We were freedom's foresters
on that wild morning. We trod with grace like dancers
the stage of our apprehension, with gritted teeth,
waiting for what would come out of the shadowy eaves.
Then we saw
the soldiers in the square, we smelt
the stink of the beast, and knew what we must do.

With wrath, with unshakeable determination
the people uprose.
On guard, people of Spain!
With some old pistols and our bare hands
we charged
we charged
we charged the soldiers there.

Now at last had the enemy shown his face
unmasked. No longer now
behind the veil of incense and the words of solemnity,
no longer behind the legalised titles of theft,
the enemy hid. Our brightening hopes
had forced them out undisguised to avow
their need to feed on the meat of broken lives,
to snuff the steam of simmering slums,
to alloy their gold with the blood of the poor.
Power ran openly amok in the barracks,
Greed took the glove from its leprous fingers in the square.
Two worlds stood face to face.

Now you behold the people, fascists; what do you say to us?
Now you have heard the people, fascists; why are you silent?

Rise up, morning of July the Twentieth,
burn up into the sky of history.
Rise up, old sun, never to be forgotten,
and let the people speak.

Tear down the oppressors.
Tear down the forts of stone with our bare hands.
Smash with our bare hands
the iron door of greed.
Open the sluice-gates of time
and let the irrigating waters flow.

We found an odd gun,
we brought it up on a truck from a beer-factory.
We rushed the Montana barracks
with some old pistols and out bare hands
through the swivelling machine-gun fire.
I was there.
I saw the officers cowering,
their faces chalked with fear.

I rose from the bed of my wife's young body
at the call of Liberty.
O feed with my blood our flag's red flame.
Comrades, remember me.

The fascists shot my children first,
they made me stand and see.
O dip the flag in my heart's blood.
Comrades, remember me.

Spain rose up in the morning,
roused by the bluster of bullets.

Unbreakfasted, the people
put the fascists to rout.
Spain rose up in the morning,
Spain rose up in the morning,
Spain rose up in the morning,
and drove the fascists out.

Therefore they came with Moors deceived and bribed,
therefore they came with Foreign Legion scum.
The fascist war-plot opened, with aeroplane-whirr,
it pockmarked Spain with spouting craters of bombs.
Mussolini the gangster rapped out his murder-instructions.
Hitler the gambler rattled his loaded dice,
to crush the people of Spain.

Therefore they shot the workers at Badajoz,
gouged and scourged and maimed and lamed and murdered,
blew up with grenades the wounded in hospital-wards,
mangled and hanged and flogged and smashed and ravished,
a fist of force slogging at every heartbeat
over the people of the invaded districts.
The rotary-presses of the world's frightened masters
champed day and night with the stereotyped lies of hate,
to crush the people of Spain.

But the workers, going to battle,
went as to fiesta.

Now is no time for tenderness
when the heart grows most tender.
Now when the whole love of a life
brims into the farewell-kiss.
We kiss with closed eyes as the train-whistle jags us.
Darling, darling, your tear-wet lashes
brush my cheeks, and then the gust of war
wrenches us apart like a leaf torn
from its tree of safety and blown headlong
into autumn. A cold wind slides
along the grinding rail-tracks of departure.
Time and the carriage-door slam between us.
The train foreshortens, concertinas into distance,
into the lifted hills of menace,
Samosierra Front,
the screech of bullets in the splayed bush of heat,
like cigarras in remembered olive-groves of home,
the phenic acid gas in murmuring tent glooms
when Juan's breast-wound bubbles,
and the sun's great hammer clanging
in the sickles of the skies,
and the shadow of the wings of death
flickering over Spain.
Toledo in the splintering rain of destruction,
in a twisted skein of tempest-light,
with time a tower of toppling stone.
Irun a town pulled down on the heads of heroes
to give them a fitting grave.

The scarred flanks of Oviedo
where miners blast their way through death's thicket.
The ruined homestead where through the window
the dying man still fires.
The cornered peasants who fight to the end,
shooting from whited holes in the cemetery-walls.

And then the flails of the chilly wind
the spikes of pain in the stark midnight watch.
We lie in coffin-grooves of rock and shoot,
while winter flaps and howls
and rides us with cruel spurs.

Yet we cry louder than the winds of darkness,
louder than all the fields of frenzy
gashed with the flame-flowers of grenades.
Hammer of industry, strike down those who would steal from us.
Sickle of plenty, cut down those who would starve us.

Mourn for the workers fallen at Badajoz
when night flows on us and the cold stars bubble,
in that dark width of silence, drown, go down,
mourn for the workers fallen, the best sons of Spain.
Mourn for the workers fallen Seville
in that dark pause that makes dark earth a stone
graven with the names of our beloved dead,
go down into the dark earth, remember them,
mourn for the workers fallen before Madrid,
mourn for the workers fallen at Malaga
mourn for the women's bodies quenched like broken moons
mourn for the children their lives snapt at flowertime
mourn for the workers fallen before Irun
their strong hands claspt upon the last defiance
their sinewy bodies gay with all freedom's promise,
wasted defaced thrust down from the lap of summer
mourn for the workers fallen the best sons of Spain.

Foreward, the sudden command jerks.
Extend in skirmishing order,
into the storm of death, the filth of pain,
into the stunning cyclone barbed with beaks of metal,
recalling only
tear-wet lashes that brushed my cheeks
and the voice that cried out over Spain:
They shall not pass!

That cry broke round the world; its tides of power
foamed upon every shore of man. The workers
answered; the International Brigade
swung through the streets of torn Madrid.
Shoulder to shoulder stood
the workers of all lands.

Therefore, dropped from a throbbing sky,
with venom of flame the snakes of death leaped jagged
among the women and children of Madrid.
Therefore the fascists gathered in greater numbers,
Hitler the gambler tosses for his world-war.
On every front of thought,
in every street dark with the stench of hunger,
in every house throughout the world
where the loudspeakers of capitalism blare,
the fascists fight this war
to crush the people of Spain.

For the war in Spain is war for the human future.
All that crawls evil out of the holes of the past,
and all that rises with love for the lucid warmth of the day,
meet in this grapple. In it meet
the evil and the good that swarm
in your inherited blood.
Yes, yours, and yours, and yours.

Listen, comrades,
if you would know our pride.
Have you ever faced your deepest despair?
Then what you see in the agony of Spain
is your own body crucified.

Listen, comrades,
of you would know our pride.
Can you dare to know your deepest joy,
all that is possible in you?
Then what you see in Spain's heroic ardour
is your own noblest self come true.

Then, workers of the world, we cry:
We who have forged our unity on the anvil of battle,
we upon whom is concentrated
the shock, the breath of flame
belched from the hell of greed,
we who are pivot of all things since we give
to-day the ground of courage and devotion,
the fulcrum of power to shift the harried world
into the meadows of the future's plenty,
we who have claimed our birthright, O hear our call.

Workers of the world, unite for us
that bear the burden of all.
You shall not hear us complain
that the wolves of death are ravening in our streets,
if you but understand, if your bodies flow
into this steel of resistance, this welded mass,
making you one with us, and making us
unconquerable.
Workers,
drive off the fascist vultures gathering
to pick the bones of Spanish cities,
to leave the Spanish fields
dunged with peasant dead
that greed may reap the fattened crops.
Fuse your unity in the furnace of our pain.

Enter this compact of steel,
and then we shall not complain.

On guard for the human future!
On guard for the people of Spain!

Requiem Mass for Englishmen Fallen in the International Brigade

Call out the rollcall of the dead, that we,
the living, may answer, under the arch of peace
assembled where the lark's cry is the only shrapnel,
a dew of song, a skywreath laid on earth
out of the blue silence of teeming light
in this spring-hour of truce prefiguring
the final triumph, call upon them proudly
the men whose bones now lie in the earth of freedom.

Stand out on the crag of morning to sound reveille.
Hark to the peal of silence, remembering.
This moment of honour claps our hearts with the future,
and already we taste, like wedlock in a first kiss,
the hour when the last barricades of estrangement
fall and the roaring battle-dusk is beaconed
with pledges of kinship, the workers world-united,
world without end, the dawn on the earth of freedom.

Ask of the eagle that yelped overhead
where in the blaze of death the Spanish workers blocked
the Guadarrama passes with their dead.
Eagle of Spain, from your eyrie of the skies
answer. Where are they now, the young and the brave?
The brotherly dead pour out of the bugle-call.
Where are the faces we seek, the English faces?
Let the living answer the rollcall of the dead.

Where now is he, gay as the heart of spring
rich with the world's adventure, wandering from where the moon
hangs in a crooked willow of Samara
to where congested London clots with a toxin
England's aorta-vein? In strength of pity,
as he had lived, he died, and the bullets whined
through boughs of winter over his broken face.
Where is Ralph Fox of Yorkshire?

Where now is he, the eager lad who beheld
England's fate whitening under Huesca's moon?
Where the shells splash enormous flowers of destruction,
flame-gawds of madness, fountain-plumes of terror,
there must freedom walk or the earth is surrendered
to these her ravishers, so I shall walk with freedom
and after the agony you will pluck fruits in the garden.
Where is John Cornford of Cambridge?

Where now is he, a voice among many voices,
who said: In poverty's jail are bolted the guiltless,
the thieves lock up their victims. His voice protested.
Sentenced, he saw through a stone-wall the truth.
Clearer that wall of privation than any arguments.
He struck his hand on the stone and swore he would break it,
he took a rifle and broke through that wall in Spain.
Where is Wilf Jobling of Chopwell?

Where now is he that amid the grinding of plates
in the trampsteamer's fo'castle listened. The waters
streamed through the hawserpipe; the ship dipped shuddering.
He learned who was racketing, who had rigged orders to gain
the world's insurance-money while drowning the crew.
Bearing an ambulance-stretcher among the trenches of danger,
I have found my way home, he answered before Madrid.
Where is Davidovich of Bethnal Green?

Where now is he that came early to fighting?
In Sydney, while gulls screamed round pinchgut, he learned,
resisting eviction, that the people were all evicted
from the world of their making and stamped into hardship's hovels.
He came back, a stowaway, to Edinburgh,
but cried: I stand in the open bows of purpose
journeying to Spain where the people claim their birthright.
Where is Jack Atkinson of Hull?

Over the faint blue streak of the sierras,
the bare scarps heaving ribbed and flattening vague
when noon scoops out the shadows from ravines,
rasped the Caproni planes. Is this a strange country,
you Scotsman? No, I have recognised it. See,
the village-children clench their fists in welcome,
for we are they in whom love becomes justice.
Where is James Wark of Airdrie?

Where now is he, that leader of London busmen,
in ragged olivegroves on the Jarama sector,
a company-commander? Wiping grit from his eye,
he laughed, and swung the machinegun on the ledge
of toppling Fascists, then to the higher ground
ordered his men. The fiery rocks split flailing
and the barrage shogged battering up the hill.
Where is Bill Briskey of Dalston?

Where now is he, that comrade quick with laughter?
Behind the sandbags he crawled with bleeding knees,
sweat blurred the pounding distance, still he fired,
the claws of heat were fastened in his arm
that scraped along the stone. A wallowing roar
fire-drenching billowed. As he was borne away,
dying, he sang the International.
Where is Alan Craig of Maryhill?

Tanks lurched up over the rise, and men from their hands and knees
flung forwards on the gust of attack staggering
head-down. Our riflefire's long crackle was drowned,
The booming rocked and racked the earth, but wavering
the crumpled line stumbled on grass-tussocks,
clumsily pitching. Out of the trench we rushed
the tanks wheeled crunching. But where is he that led us?
Where is Robert Symes of Hampshire?

Where now is he that, tramping on means-test marches,
knew that the road he had taken against oppression
led to the front in Spain? For he was marching
in country lined with harlot-hoardings of menace,
England seared into slums by the poison-bombs of greed.
That road of anger and love must lead to Spain,
the shouts in Trafalgar Square to No pasaran.
Where is Tommy Dolan of Sunderland?

This war has roots, everywhere, in the soil of squalor.
He watched on the tarnished slates the glistening moon,
a milky drip of light mocking the mouth of hunger,
a promise of cleansing beauty, a pennon of freedom;
and midnight, yawning, creaked with the ghosts of old pain,
till resolution regathered like the moonlight flowing
in through the cast iron bars at the foot of the bed.
Where is T.J. Carter of West Hartlepool?

As summer is plighted in the little red cones of larch,
so will the fullness of freedom unfold from these,
our comrades, in its hour. For unless the onset
of spring was here in the spears of daffodil
and eyes of the sticklebacks emerald in water-darkness,
no summer breath would gloss the plum or ruffle
the hill's gold harvest-fur. And so we cry:
Where is Sid Avner of Stoke Newington?

These men as types of the English dead in Spain
we summon here in this nested hush of the spring
rising amid grey clouds of travellers-joy,
with marshgold smouldering in the hollows of sunset,
and sweetness plaited in the hazel-catkins.
Here in this green hawthorn-moment of England,
we conjure them, brief as an azure drift of windflowers,
and lasting as the earth of unity.

Soldiers

Looked at from across the fence, what are they?
Men, drab-clothed, sweating at some fatigue, and somehow
cut off from the life you know. The cheery voices
may cross that barrier, and you too may answer,
but cannot enter. There is a centre here
excludes you, and a meaning in the voices,
beyond the words, you may hear but nor interpret.

I too saw them like that, across the fence,
until the day I put their drabness on
and entered. It was different from my thought.
I had not thought at all, I had watched excluded,
but now was on the other side and answered,
and the meaning in the voices now was simple,
nothing to shout about, but a shared warmth.

Soldiers tramping amid the plumes of dust,
putting a bren together in record time,
blood-blistering a thumb, waiting on schemes
close to the ramp for the grating on the pebbles,
polishing buttons or chatting in mess-room queues,
inside your voices, strengthens in the handclasp
you have no time to think, but a meaning gathers
In the dank Nissen, around the parked truck,
under the gun-nets, the eyes drowse and the voices
stumble, and no word has yet been found
to utter the thought. against fascism we fight.
The Atlantic Charter. Unity. We the people.
Jazz-beats slap the heart with a home-yearning.
When the next man sings, those are the songs he sings.

There is another day, of the shaken earth:
light-clap, flame-spout, thunder-splash corrosive
on face and hands, all the pomps and grime of terror.
Against the sheeted fire I see them moving.
O friend with blood pouring from your finger-nails,
broken body of man stark on the flare of agony,
O face of my friend bloodily blinded, gone.

The slogans pass, across the dusk of musing,
and are not yet our thought, which slips away.
Suddenly the anger speaks but confusedly.
Suddenly the love breaks open, but is too shy.
And yet we know. We know where our anger goes,
and what we love, and we now that the day will come
when there will be words for this anger and this love.
And yet it is happening all the while. We know it.
Act becomes word, word becomes act. It is happening.

Against Fascism.
Unity.
We the People.

Production Front

You are an Englishman.
What do you mean, saying it? Say it.
I am an Englishman.
What does it mean?
What does it mean today?

Men speak of freedom.
Men speak of the struggles that gained our freedom.
It is written in books.
It is used to give a flourish
to the speeches of politicians
and the leading-articles of newspapers.

There are shadowy figures
and the broken echo of trumpets
from the valley of lost causes.

There are shadowy figures
bending over your lives,
and you have names, perhaps, for some of them,
and some of the names flash an allegiance.
You are grateful,
not quite knowing why,
but you are grateful,
you know, but don't know why,
you owe the good of your lives
to men whose names are flags
on the stricken field of history,
glittering yet across the litter of years
amid the unyielding echo of those trumpets.

Somehow you know that what you feel of fullness,
of life lived strongly to the full,
springs from those shadowy figures
to whom the word Freedom
was instant in the heart's core,
was clang of a loyalty obeyed at once and always,
was light in the inmost crannies,
a song of courage in the cells of oppression
and a sword in the streets of struggle.

How bring those shadowy figures
out of the starry darkness
into the stark light of your daily lives,
make them share your closest needs,
aid your hope of a life enriched
and a decent world for your children?
These giant figures
cloudy on the mountaintops of history,
how bring them, with a handshake,
into your kitchen, into the pub-bar?
into your factory, workshop, mine?
They can enter, they are friendly,
you have spoken with them
and have not recognised their voices.
They have stood beside you,
they stand beside you now.

Remember the first kiss
of the girl you love.
If you are married, remember
the day and night of your marriage.
Can you remember it?
It's not so easy to remember.
O life the lovely river
burst there at full flood,
burst the settled banks,
burst from the heart of fullness
into the meadows of a new life.

Remember the first day
you went to work.
You stepped from familiar bonds
of safety, stepped
from the warmth of the hearth-circle
into a new sphere of authority
flapped with cold winds and fears of failure,
and did not fail, but got your grip
and found a place in the widening world of action.
Can you remember it?
It's not so easy to remember.

O life the mighty river
carried you on its crest,
carried you from the sheltered pool of home
into the world of work,
into the hurry and swirl of great water,
into the clasp of a brotherly union,
the great tide sweeping on.

Freedom is no different.
It is not built on another shore
with the trumpets sounding from the further side.
It is not a dream of fiery figures
cloudy on the hills of sunset.

It is close as love and work,
closer than breathing,
born from the generations
of men and women no different from yourselves,
born from this generation,
inherited, preserved or lost by you,
you that listen here.

Now as always, it is the ceaseless flow
linking a man with his fellows,
knitting you to man. Goes quicker beside you
than your blown shadow. The innermost flame of the flame
kindling you man. Freedom.

Think of it like that.
Not as a vague word, perhaps a blind,
not as a shadowy tumult,
but as the quickening of your spirit,
the second birth, the song cleaving discord,
the sudden song, the simple pulse of love,
blossom of your blood and deepmost leap
of laughter, the quiet joke, the resolving touch,
the shared pillow, the meeting eyes of friendship,
the homing call of children in the dusk,
the triumphant swell of music,
movements of men at work,
endless movements of men at work,
men linked by work, men linked all over the world
by needs and purposes of work,
work transforming the world,
completing mastery over nature,
defeating the old wolves of famine and fear.

That is Freedom.
Not something distant, not a distant brightness
and calling of martyrs ravished out of time.
Freedom has been with you all your days,
your days and nights. The inherited struggle
netting your every act. Is speaking here.
Freedom.
The drive of the break-through.
It sang in the deep of love, and it sings there.
It clenched in the thick of work, and is clenched there.
That energy breaking through.
Breaking through into fullness.
You have known it in your own struggles.
It is no different in the surge of history.
There it is your life twined with a million others
all facing the same needs and purposes.
Freedom is the break-through
into the new union.
What then the need today?

Black on your lives,
black on England, black on all the world,
the fascist menace hangs its toppling thundercrag.
There stands the barrier.
All that you touch in love,
all the union and ending of fear,
all that you hold in work,

the promise of plenty and the gay mirrors
where life rejoices in herself,
all, all is menaced, thwarted, doomed
unless the fascist threat is met and broken.
There is the point where we must make
the break-through, freedom, or we fail,
utterly fall. O that is why
our victory unbolts all doors to joy and plenty,
defeat makes certain the dearth and the dark
and the death of all that gives your life its worth.

Now some must move upon that wall of terror
and walk through heaving stone and bristling fires of steel.
Your to make possible that advance.
Striking this blow at fascism, in your hand
grips all the past of struggle, our English struggle.

All the shadowy figures become real
in clatter of hammers or machinegun fire –
aimed at this enemy's overthrow;
in harvesting sickles and gunfire swivelling.
Increase production.
In mine and factory, shipyard and foundry,
at lathe or assembly line, kilnflare or vat,
work to the beat of that purpose and need.
Increase production.
Love's pulse the pulse of that need of delivery.
Work's urge the urge of that purpose of union,
the purpose of break-through.

That is the meaning of struggle
one with our lives. Understand
as a single and irreconcilable anger
the meaning of this war.
Soldier, fight.
Worker, work,
for the break-through,
the ending of fascism,
all energies linked for that purpose,
the break-through, the ending of fascism,
in unity of labour and battle,
weld all purposes, turn to your work,
saying: I know it.
I am an Englishman.
I know what it means, saying today:
I am an Englishman.

Peace is our Answer

1   She Began No Wars

Look closely. Has this woman your own face?
Is she your mother, is she your daughter, moaning?
Is she your wife? Lift up the darkness
of her fallen hair, and ask again:
Whose face looks in between the broken stones?
whose face of haunted pain?

This night of all night any night tonight
the walls may fall, the flames may claim your bones,
the stones, less stubborn than our bodies, crack
under the thunder, falling.
This face looks in through every pane of fear –
Answer! Whose voice is calling?

2   Who Will Dare Look This Child In The Eyes?

This leprosy of death, this delicate
device of pain as vast as a star gone rotten
with some shrewd virus of decay:

This intricate defilement of deepest springs,
this pus of death that blotches and blots the sun
across the pitted face of day:

This thing was made by man, his brain, his hands.
You are a man, accomplice of this Thing.
Redeem your birthright while you may.

Hell has another name now, Hiroshima,
darker than all the rings of burning darkness
where Dante clambered his accusing way.

Can you escape the ghosted night, the eyes
of children scraped to ragged bone?
You are a man. What word have you to say?

3 Who Drives Them On?

The fugitives of fear
carry fear in the blood.
They flee in a night of fear
and the night is all around.
Each thought is the fin of a wave
lost in the tumbling flood.
They seek for boundaries
in a world with no bound.

When no question is asked,
who may answer back?
The dumb must find voices,
the deaf hear each other's cries.
The boundary is here,
where the fugitive halts in his track.
The fear is gone when he looks
his neighbour in the eyes.

4   There Is No Escape

Deep in the night of the earth
mother and children lie.
Who has stolen away the stars
from their havening sky?

Who has snatched the carpet of grasses
from under their feet?
Who has knotted the wreaths of venom
where flowers were sweet?

Who has spiked the rattling leaves
against their thin hands?
Who has quenched the gold moon of the lovers
and darkened all lands?

Earth is not deep enough
or the caves of the sea.
No tears will deter the murderers,
no human plea.

They will be powerless
when their power is broken.
They will be silenced
when the people have spoken.

5   They Think That Freedom Can Be Jailed

Here is the end of the world.
The barbed-wire marks the plain abyss,
the death of man,

the death of all that has proudly made a man
in pang of aspiration,
since the precarious fires began.

The eyes of the stars are all prickled out with pins.
The screams that weal the bloody darkness
serve but to deepen the eternal silence,

the death of man, the arctic hush of murder.
There is no further death than this.
Here is the end of the world.

Yet here, where only jagged and barren stones
slope to the abject precipice,
even here, the spirit of man survives and answers.

Under the breath of silence runs the song
of brotherhood. The clang of prisoned feet
chimes with the hearts of hope in other lands
where men are free to build against the dawn.

Yes, here in darkness clotted and withdrawn
freedom is clenched within the fettered hands,
the pulse of song preserves its angry beat,
and the heart echoes still: How long, how long?

6   The Factory of Death

In the deepest night
he stands alone.
On the reeking trees
the sparks are blown,
the smuts of flesh,
the scales of bone.

The helpless man
with his hands tied,
whipped and wounded
in the side,
with splintered ribs:
where may he hide?

Still to and fro
with prison pace –
O see yourself
in that dark place,
meeting evil
face to face.

The terrible shame
that men can fall
so low. The pity
panged over it all,
furnace-belch
and blood-soaked wall.

In the deepest night,
in the heart of stone,
the smoke of flesh,
he lies alone.
Can you understand?
Can you atone?

7   The Scared Men

The faces change,
the faces are still the same.
You pass in the street today
then men who crucified Christ,
the men who thrust your brother
into the Auschwitz-flame,
the same one or another
who plays the ravening game
with all things bought and sold,
all murderously priced.

They are afraid,
these man of the ruthless hour,
who will wreck the world with a grin
rather than slacken their hold.
The atom-bomb that they nurse
is their greed in its ultimate flower:
their rule is wholly a curse,
destruction their only power,
World-end the last toss of their coin
for an earth that is bought and sold.

8   The People Have an Answer

The Sun, as a leader of the resistance,
under the eyes of policemen sprinkles
golden leaflets along the distance
and slips gay posters on every wall.
The people gather at the call.

Life against Death: the choice is simple,
but only simple folk can make it.
Men who are tied to the deathworld trample
the propagandist flowers and slight
the manifesto of the light.

Now peace is one with Life, we answer,
one with the buxom earth of Plenty.
Peace is the poise of the proud dancer,
the wheat that shrugs in the combing breeze,
the cloud of birds in the morning trees,

the steel-light roaring from the ladle,
the turbine pulsing in the mountain,
the breasts of milk above the cradle,
the hands of lovers in the dark,
the wings of song that brush the park.

And now the Speeches are amplifying
echoes of park and home and workshop.
High over London the voice is crying,
and deep in the heart it enters in.
For Peace is Life, and Life must win.

9   Here Peace Begins

The grass upthrusts in souring earth
through rusted bedsteads in the yard.
The red geranium on the sill
defies the grime. And on the hearth
the child is bred with sturdy will.
For life is good, and life is hard.

Union they know at its full worth
because the struggles never cease;
and that's a lesson to repeat.
Death they know, and they know Birth.
Ban the Bomb from Market Street!
Mothers are demanding Peace!

10   Peace Has 400,000,000 Names

Here the tumultuous centre:
the eddies flurry,
break in or break away,
and the centre grips.
Still gossiping is Nell,
but Jane's a shopper,
and Mary doesn't mind
whatever at all.

Into equality enter,
dawdle or hurry,
it's merry and market-day,
and the quack with his quips
holds Mary in his spell,
Nell comes a cropper,
and Jane still cannot find
the winkle-stall.

Here is the centre steady
through every rambling eddy:
Sign the Petition!
Here on the rickety table
you too are able
to master nuclear fission.

Your name's not blurred, submerged,
when you have signed.
The others enlarge your life
and surge behind.
Millions of hands
clench in your hand
millions of minds
sing in your mind.

11 Who Is Against Peace?

Banners of sunlight flap along
the roadways where the people throng,
who know the discipline of song.

They call and chat across the files,
marching the slow fraternal miles
to Hyde Park or the Blessed Isles.

The Sunday silence of the street
duly records the tramp of feet
and slogans that the hearts repeat.

There's somebody who hates the song,
there's somebody who thinks it wrong,
and he is many policemen strong.

A baton breaks the singing spheres,
a child is lost and bursts in tears,
a man goes on amid the cheers,

the hooves are trampling round the place,
a policeman leans with snarled grimace,
a man goes down with broken face,

placards are trodden in the mud,
a woman screams with hands of blood,
the batons swing, the batons thud,

The streets – to whom do they belong?
To him, it seems, who hates the song,
a man who's many policemen strong.

But will he own the streets for long?

12 We are Many They Are Few

Who tosses free the doves of dawn that fly
to every heart, to every bough of sky –
that circle round the world and bless all lands,
and then come homing to the open hands?

They rise wherever men have stood
for life and found the struggle good,
wherever common men are met
angry at the darkening threat,

wherever, careless of derision,
men are true to the gay vision:
O the blinding bondage breaks
and the light of hope awakes.

and under the crack of torture still
sings the clear unravished will
and from slums where the children cry
the brotherhoods of song march by.

Peace is a country to be won
by you and me, and everyone.
To reach its frontiers we shall need
all our thews of word and deed.

Every murderous lie dispelled,
every aggressive act that's held,
every weapon of war withdrawn,
is another step towards the dawn.

And we are those who free its doves to fly
to every heart, to every bough of sky –
to circle round the world and bless all lands,
and come home nesting to our open hands.

Cry of Greece: A Mass Declamation

Turning to England out of the thorns of our shadow
we look on averted faces and hurrying backs.
To whom shall we plead now? and who will answer us?
Who hears the crackle of deaths and the tears of the children
that sound whenever the name of Greece is spoken?

Call down the hawks of the sun with the tinkling of tears
call up the sea's bubble-monsters with flowerbells of dew
wear down the mountain-boulders with tumbling of lovers.
All that is easy to the softening of closed hearts.
To whom shall I sing then, who come with a song of pity?

To whom I shall I sing then, who come with a song of glory?
A song that should waken a tumult of answering wings
come with a snarl of trumpets and lifted laughters
come with a clap of the morning-stars for its echo.
To whom shall we sing here our songs of pity and glory?

I am afraid, and stand in a fire-ring of sorrows.
Where are the voices? where is that pride of high musicks?
where are the English voices? the eagles of tempest?
where are the trumpets lusty against the liars?
I have no heart to call in the darkening silence.

Yet if one man stands at bay against all the darkness
there shall be stars, a swarm of unquenchable stars.
If one man stands at bay against all the silence
there shall be voices O bladed voices unsheathed.
I am standing at bay against silence of death and the darkness.
I bring you a song of the Greeks on the hills of hunger.
I bring you a song of the Greeks in the perilous passes
a song of pity, a stubborn song of glory.
Flash out, courageous sword on the crag of the day.
Cry out, voices of children, the endless pang.

Hard is the stone of the heart and guilt is a deafening hush.
We shall split the stone of the heart with a voice from beyond the horizon:
The moan of the Greek children grows round your moated homes.
The Greek women are ravisht each night in the bed of your love.
At the foot of your garden hangs the crucified man
who trusted you, the Greek, brave heart the most betrayed.

I saw the mountains moving, and the sky
sagging with planes, the rasping fall of the stars
and earth with many fangs. The Germans came
and we fought back. O land of the gnarled olive
against the golden dust and the winedark seas
we fought, we had no hope of victory then
we fought. Remember Forty-One. Strain back
behind the jangling lies, the mists of murder.

If you have any love for angry truth
if you have ever sheltered the small flame of love
inside your helpless hands against the storm of the world
O think again of that shared exaltation and its faiths
and tear a husk of cruelty from the sun
that darkens all our hearts. Stark earth of Greece
set with a great carven stones and a strip of maize
between the rags of hill and the shining waters,
our land, we fought, and had no hope of victory.
We fought beside you and we hoped for victory
but never thought what blow would bring us down
what blow struck from behind O English brothers:
whose name and power were invoked to strike us down?

There as we stood in the trust of our first rejoicing
we were taken and thrust in the barbedwire sties and the cells
set on the desolate islands of grinding light
lashed and ravished in the police-stations
shot in the thickets, shot in the quayside alleys.

The Fascists were back in the Ministries, pacing the carpets
the Fascists were back in the clanking courts of the law
behind the grilles of the bank and the rings of cigar smoke
in the grand hotels and the dancing, the cocktail bars,
and all of their screechbright women with nylon flesh

Whose were the bayonets guarding the quick change-over?
Whose were the warships riding our restless waters?
Whose were the troops preserving the murderous order?
Whose then the hand of ultimate choice and control?
Answer, people of England, the voice of our dead.

We fought again, who have always fought. We fought
along the mountain-ridges and the caves of shadow
with scythes and stones and the bare fists of a man
and then with the good weapons that we'd captured
we fought and are fighting and will always fight.

Whose are the bayonets guarding the government decrees?
whose are the ships that come with the fascist aid?
whose are the men that sail to the sad Peiraeus?
whose are the generals and economic advisors
chatting in Athens, plotting in Salonika?

Answer, people of England, the voice of our dead.
Answer the voice of your own dead who fought
beside us and are one now with our spirit.
Answer the sigh of your loved-one and your children
pledges of peace and an earth of brotherly plenty,
answer the dead man standing at your side.

Answer, people of England, our common dead.
What sent the world wrangling in wrongs and rankling
when the war ended and all of us hoped to be happy?
The murder seething in the pit of Greece
the treachery splitting Greece with fears and famines
the breaking of faith. That broke the hopes of all.

Here lies the cause of all our woe and here
the chance of clear redemption and of peace.
Greece is the open sore of imperialist evil.
When the Greeks are free, all over Europe again
the unity of the peoples will be possible.

There is no avoiding of this responsibility
People of England, look in on your own hearts:
The moan of the Greek children grows round your moated homes
The Greek women are ravisht each night in the bed of your love.
At the foot of your garden hands the crucified man
who trusted you, the Greek, brave heart the most betrayed.

We bring you a song of the Greeks on the hills of hell.
We bring you a song of the Greeks in the perilous passes
a song of pity, a stubborn song of glory.
Flash out, courageous sword on the crag of the day.
When Greece is free, the shadow will pass away.
Peace will be in our hands. Peace will be strong.
O open your hearts to the hands of our beating song.
Let Greece be free again. Let Greece be free.

Buffalo Stadium, Paris, 1948

to Paul Eluard

If all the winds of the heavens
that have blown through the crannies of time
were gathered within one valley
and clashed in a single tumult

If all the Springs of the earth
that have woken man with a song
were gathered within one garden
and burst in a single blossom

If all the notes of the birds
that have shaken the crystal bough
were gathered inside one silence
and rose in a single rapture

this day in Paris
this day everywhere

I see men coming from the dust of distance
winding about the sides of toppling mountains
and past their dearths and deaths, their daze of danger
they look towards this day

I see young lovers stooping from last night
under the mornings arch with secret laughters
to face the world without the need of veils
and move within this day

I see the peoples mated with the harvest
awakening from the night of stolen labour
to claim their birthright at the sun's tribunals
and move within this day

this day in Paris
this day everywhere

All that man is and all that man has been
meet gaily with the man who is yet to be
and march to the tune of the song in which I join

all the winds of the heavens
all the springs of the earth
all the notes of the birds
gathered in a single hand, in a single heart

This day in Paris
this day everywhere
catching in its handclasp
all days that have been, all days that are yet to be

We look in each other's eyes
and see the babe of the newlife there
cradled in inner light

We look out on the world and ask:
why did it take so long to find this place
where no one casts a shadow?

This day whose date is unity
this day with its red seal on the charter of man

Paul, this day is yours
Through the arch of your poems march
the people to this tryst
this oval space of truth.

The shaken diamond shadows of maidenhair
under the waterfall-spray
are less gentle than the trembling of your fingers
as they inscribe this day among your poems.

There are not many poets blest so fully.
Mayakovsky hearing the boots of sailors hammer
his metres on the cobbles of Leningrad
was not so proudly tall.

The poet sang of a single love.
Then looking up he saw about him gathered
in tiers on tiers of silence the myriad eyes
the stars and all men living.

Pablo Neruda at Stalingrad, 1949

1   We Were on our Way to the Tractor Factory

We were on our way to the Tractor Factory.
We stopped the car and walked by the zigzag cracks,
the oddments of war washt clean of their blood by the rain
and the harsh wind licking the straggled bushes.

We crossed a railway bridge. And I watched him bend
and take some shrapnel out of the ribs of the earth.
Later we chugged across the Volga
and swam in the great waters, and in my head
the moment remained. That and the sense of cleansing,
the sky that was sky upon sky, the hurdling sweep of the river
and the broad steppe-wind sliding into Asia.

Neruda looked out on Stalingrad,
recognising
his own images uprising
all round him from the burnt and buckled tracks
and battered scarps, the cracks
of parched and living clay,
the rubble of steel and rusted stone.
His face was sad
with acid tangs of wormwood blown
across the rabaged day,
the stark eternal earth of Stalingrad.

Neruda looked on Stalingrad,
realising
his own images uprising,
and weighed a scrap of shrapnel in his hand,
the split transfigured land
with stubborn steel-lights spilt
on children of the unbroken dance,
his face was glad,
his song was gathered in his glance,
where spread serenely built
the green eternal city of Stalingrad.

2 Now is the Moment

You sit there rounded like an impossible Buddha
incarnated as the primordial Spaniard
blandly incorruptible as porcelain
and judging the world with total sympathy
for every known and unknown manifestation of life
and behind you are scattered the fragments of Stalingrad
with the people living still in holes in the ground
as if you had risen out of the titanic earth
five minutes after Zeus had thrown
his final dexterous thunderbolt
to settle the monsters of volcanic slime:
'Now is the moment we must create the world afresh.'

Your wife is smiling subtly at your side
thinking of something quite different
but as necessary
in the summer light of her irrepressible eyes,
something expressed in the fine contours of her cheeks.
She turns to you without turning.

Afterwards I swam in the turbulent Volga
and fought the waters, afraid of drowning
while you benignly regarded the sunset earth,
remarking as I emerged
shuddering in the heat:
'This day has been longer than any day can be.'

Three Letters to Nikolai Tikhonov

Autumn

How are you faring in that Other World
with the white of mountain snow on your fiery hair
and a bristly sun at your heel whisks at a whistle
to dig you a golden grotto of Georgian warmth

you in the oval core of a crystal grape
like a lover in a lover's pupil reflected
in a lover's pupil whole as a spark of dew.

How are you faring in that Other World?

I am cold this morning in the tassel-tags of mist,
the year slips through my hands and the jagg'd boughs,
and the brown river is crowned with the twists of foam
in a silence broken by the water vole's splash
in a silence receding into the cavern of reeds
where something turns over and over and dies again

and the grey squirrel peers through the open fingers
of bony oak twigs. Only last night a rat
gnawed hungrily at the lintel of my door
and all night sank in my dream the precision of his tooth.
Then with the east of the morning I looked to the east.

Send me a slip of your sun to plant by my waters
and break my windows with the red stone of your laugh.

*

Yours is a world that's bursting through a world
like fruit from flower in a brief hour.

Yours is a world that's closing round a world
a fist of light that tightens
breaking the ancient locks of the measured seed

to loose the seed within the seed
to fuse the fist of light with the honeying fruit
to see within the fruit the pip of the ungrown tree
the tree in the pip and the flower in the tree
with all the blue fires of the children's hair
crisping along the shadow of the green
a million years ahead and now

It's always now
now in your laughter breaking the smoky windows
with a horn of wine and a dove from the steel fountains.

*

Two songs may meet above the flight of eagles.
Send up your song and I shall send up mine
above the tallest crag your snow has rounded
the span of your wings will help me across the gap

and there in the golden leaves of the ungrown tree
we'll rifle the moons of milk and the merry mouths
and then return upon our different worlds
with the same candid juices the same maddening sweetness
the mountain-echoes of songs of the unborn children.

*

And you will sing more happily lapped at home
by the singing river and the wise seed begetting
wheat and rose on the selfsame stalk. And I
shall sing entranced and mad as a maenad of stone
in the gardens of trespass where the rain is black
and lovers go seeking for unforgotten selves
in the thorns of their tears and their unavailing deaths

till at a tiptoe kiss
they hear the beat of the silence caverned in my tree
that takes the note of each wrangled life and echoes it in a concord,
and suddenly see their faces burning in the mirror of the rose
and know the cheat that's shut them out from their own bodies always
even at a tiptoe kiss.

They will claim with their ghostly hands the hands of earth,
by the glow of that kiss their long lost mouths will come home,
they will pass through each other's body into their own,
and turn again on the wrath-point of a grace
branched from the dance that sparks in the round of the grape
where you are globed with a song of eternal life

and that's the moment when Capitalism dies
and lovers and workers are one in the cock of the dawn.

They will be born again
with the sky of a storm in their hands and their righteous hair
and the shell of Venus curved blue in their halcyon eyes
and the face of Marx grown one with the ancient stones.

*

Lovers, look up and see the dove
flash on the edge of your new sight
above the man of hills you never saw before
where Time has found new curves of stillness:
that was the song of my friend
going down to Moscow.

And now I know the silence where it nests
in the nook of that tall future which stands rooted
in our scummed river and scurfing leaves of mist
as well as in fields of the gold gay Ukraine
where amid the bells of summer I saw men sowing
a double seed of rye and song in the furrows

gathered before the dawn in a harvest of honeys
under green orchard-stars in the ring of the laughters
where the accordion swings with its ribbons
wide as the steppe-horizon:
Swing high, accordion-player,
making an arch of music for the moon.

For here is the earth at last, a place long dreamed-of
seen by the poets when they closed their eyes
and always lost to the people. Here at last
safe in the shaping hands and nightly discovered
under the dancing feet in the meadow of apples.

Call to all lost crazed sailors. Earth at last!
After a malice of storms, with bilge and worms-meat
after listless muttering months of fever
and toils without a chart, ho, Earth at last,
Earth on the skyline, Earth in the spirit's waters
upheaving in shaggy hills and the fountains of trees
veined with the fire's blood
tossing up birds to the skies.

Tell it to the lovers, tell it to poets, in secret.
Shout it to workers in worlds where the walls are iron
hammered to murderous spikes or a rusty smoke
bitter across the eyes. For here is the dancing,
here is the Earth:

Swing high, accordion-player,
making an arch for the moon and a pearl-faced girl

till with the first long sigh of sleep
the trodden juices ooze from the vats of stone
built in the hills of distance
and burn in the dark of a dream near daybreak
burn with unbearable fires of sweetness
the earth turning
the deep calm opening and closing
valves of oceanic renewal

and wake to your world pulled down from the hoarding heavens
with a crack of corroded girders of time and space
astonishing eagles and angels

but never the deepmost heart of man.

*

Nikolai, what are you at in the Other World
alone with your hulking cat on a skiey stone
looking all round the globe and back again
to a small hearth of lichened applewood
plush with green flames and the crackle of splendid thymes
that warm your open philosophic hands
and add their energies to each dynamo purring
to light up inside your flowers with colours unknown
and scatter a sackful or two of five-pointed stars
among Lysenko's millet.
Remember me
a moment, and then forget me in a song.

Winter

What of My World then, chuckling among the beeches?
I meant to say something but the winter answered
out of its turn, with an inconsolable bird,
ahead of my mouths, and now I have lost the cue.
The echoes of my thought come back in the water
dripping from the wounded hill among the mosses.
I must listen a moment before I interpret my silence.

*

Men clap their hands before a flabby fire,
frost cribbles and spills the soil along the hill.
This weather dulls the wits, it is English weather,
a damned mouse nibbles the roof and won't stay still.

Clouds are sagging dinted on the elm tops,
the rivulet dribbles through its beard of cress.
I like this desperate pause without a clocktick,
and only the blackbird screams with a mock-distress.

*

Begin then from my hillcrest lost in mist,
a track sodden with leaves that gutters down
past the dim burning windows of the dew
and twisting oak-roots, to the ambushed town,

the pubs where songs are sunk amid the dart-scores:
England is husht, with the God of Football Pools
working out winners and getting his figures wrong
despite all the Woolworth gadgets. On stairs of the rats,
treads in the gap between two beats of the heart,
a pit of creakings, falling, rheumatic twinges
upblown in threshing and hooked sparks. Or stirs
to stare on a backyard-world too drab for devils,

and only for that reason not boarded with hoardings:
HELL TRESPASSERS WILL BE PROSECUTED
quickly no need to knock on the doors, no one expects us,
without our leaflet to-day the thoughts go nagging
the angers hungering. Here are the fumace-fires
banked in an old claypipe, and the great hammers
poised on the callous of thumb.
But now is the stink of coke, and the trick with matches,
and words we have blurted before. And so let's skirt
the derelict tips and shrouded lathes of Sunday,
the lovers refuged from rain in the telephone-booth,
and the dumb couples chained in the cinema-queue –

come back, come back to my hilltop and its mists
spouting in ghostly trees. A proper place
for apocalyptic conversations, please,
in the hush of England Winter Nineteen-fifty.
The shadows of boughs filagreed with starlight
freeze in the waters. Good.

I'll explain now why I wanted this ragged place
claimed by the owl at moonrise and the vixen
lank in the bracken when frost knocks at the tongue's root
and the fronds of smoke crumble and crack in the eyes.
The moment of dearth. I chose it for our chat
from an old emblem book, a cut of Quarles,
the budded bough splitting the Rock of death.

I want the furious comment of your laughter.
Listen. The rock unlocks its chambered toad,
the toad vomits its jewel, the jewel writes
threaded with starlights its pale cryptogram
upon the lily's ambiguous puff of shadow:

... no escape
for it is closing time
in the gardens of the West
and from now on an artist will be judged
only by
the resonance of his solitude
or the quality of his despair...

Personally I'd rather beget a brood
of irrelevant devils on a sourpuss ghost
here in this needling bed of frost than tune
the gut-strings of my decent solitude
in such an orchestra of absences

in a such a parlourgame of huddling fears
we know the Artist conjured by the charade
to play the martyred part in the petting-party
with a trim trauma tinkered to a cancer
pouting to deft resentment at being left out
of someone's something somewhere infinitely left out.

yes, certainly a bore,
then let's go home,
home but what's that?
there's no door any more,
haven't you read your sartre
on mont martre?

Yes, certainly we know this Artist resonant
as a capricorn-beetle ticking in the genitals
of some sad Brazilian, or an atlantosaurus
with nothing much in its skull but a spinal cord
three times as thick as its brain
and a prehistoric orgasm
reverberating into extinction, the nether neant.
Down Nero down:

amid a titter of teaspoons praising the desert,
amid the telephone directories praising silence,
amid the impotent fairies praising love,
between the clique and the claque praising poverty,
between the cocktail and the brandy praising renunciation
between the comma and the coma discovering integrity,

with hey for the yogi
whistling up a commissar bogey
and ho for the dope
the Absolutely Independent Intellectual,
with no hope,
no damned hope at all,
but cashing in
on the crapgame and the pope
though he keeps his conscience as clear as it's ineffectual
and believes not in Wallstreet but in Original Sin,
somehow or other it's found
Original Sin suits Wallstreet down to the ground.

He's antisoviet, of course,
an idealist rejecting force,
and so he selflessly supports
a culture based on superforts,
atomic bombs and hydrogen,
and the blasted death of man.

He's strong for freedom of the mind,
and so in all his thoughts we find
he calmly follows on behind
the press-lord's slogans well-designed
to keep the people dumb, deaf, blind.

He's strong for independent thought,
and so with claptrap pap he's caught,
and when he proudly sends abroad
the richest thought with which he's stored,
the deepest thought with which he's cored,
the echo of some dull press lord
is heard, although he tries to hide
the fact with world-end glorified.
And thus his artform justifies
the murder darkening our skies.

*

O Nikolai reaching at last your crag of snow,
up through the sweat of danger, looking down
out of the thunder of your solitude,
look down on the small furred forests of ancient hermits
who met with bloody fists their daily devils
and laughed with the glory of God.
That's an old business
and shrunken out of date, but in its darkness
not altogether shaming a race embroiled
with starspawn restless in its loins.
Look down
on the many worlds of death, the lions of fire
roaring on the iron hills, the shapeless bellies
beaked in the darkening heat and the random fangs,
golgothas of greed, the mad medusa-nations,
cloaca of the egg.
How far we have come
out of the interlocked mouths. Look down on history,
see by the terrible flares of golden blood,
the burning Sodoms of our past, that draw us
to stand and stare at last,
a weeping pillar of salt on the desolate shores,
pity and horror, blind us,
and yet we see with tears for broken eyes
out of the stark sockets. Shuddering
dies on the other side of death, we live

beyond the moment of death, and look again
on our buried hearts, the houses of the worm,
where men have made the monstrous bargains, lifting
the hem of the shadow, to buy the cold secret
of the hydra polyp or serve the tiger's writ
on the slumbering child.
For there are presences
excreting on the faces of certain men
damnation. Rise, you peoples of the world,
this last fight let us fight.

*

You know the answer. But we are chatting here
in winter's cleft, in England. Here is something
that must be seen by darkness, its own effluence
that shapes it what it is. Soon it will pass,
but first it must be faced. O my poor people,
what have they done to you?

Spring

The wind has tossed her pebble in the pond
and the tree waves her handkerchief.
A bride is waiting, in the maybush
but the mirror of silence yields no face
and I look beyond.

Trouble the waters, lily of light. A key
has turned in the quick door of green
and the day's maze encloses.
Six foot of bluebell earth, enough,
my shadow has claimed for me.

*

Now greenly like a ghost of glass
the day on the wavetop sways,
the translucent Shadow high as sky
leans to the lane's lap.

What will the drag-net dredge from the depth
after the tugging hush?
a crackt skull speaking an oracle
among the leaping fish
or a hole in the empty net and storm
coming up with a rush?

This mated moment is O of birth.
Before the wave curls past
the tree's heart breaking open reveals
the lost statue at last.

*

This spring came easily like a lily opening
in a slow motion film, with little jerks
and gentle subsidences, the ring of the waters
flickered blue to windflowers and the thrush
urged on his song like a child his rocking-horse
riding to kingdom come.

I sing the day when the people in their movements
will own this urgency and ease, will tread
with grass-roots tingling the lifted arch of the sole,
as once the peasants saw the trees releasing
naked girls in a circle, now the dancers
will enter into the trees.

*

> ...there is no escape
> for the orchard of life
> bearing twelve manner of fruits
> breaks green about us,
> and from now on the Artist will be judged
> only by
> the fullness of his communion
> and the quality of his happiness..

The Leaves of the Orchard
are for the healing of the Nations.
Nothing shall be any longer forbidden.
There shall be no more night.
There shall be no further need of torches.

I Jack saw and heard these things.
When I had heard and seen
I fell down to worship at the feet of the Angel
and the Angel was the Earth,
a great bush of singing birds
and people coming and going.
And my heart was broken with love,
my heart was whole again.

*

Light, let there be light.
Joy, let there be joy.
What meagre voice will dare
to brag of its despair
in the new earth that swings
starred from the magian east?

O from the rags of stone, the chasmed hills,
the light breaks suddenly increased
and strikes a million bells of silver,
a chime of sweetness, all the gilt spires of dew,
fire-throats of birds and apple-glints of green.
And in the heart there wells
the spellbound note victorious and serene.

O subtle power of joy
your smallest wildflower-spark
lights a great universe
and holds at bay the dark
and blasts the ancient curse.

But all despair is weak
in its smug treacheries
as a mere pebble rolled
in tremendous seas.

For joy proclaims creation
and wills the world.
In pure participation
all art is born.
But in despair
life turns away from life,
divorce of the ghost and the bone,
the man and the wife,
the deathtwist of scorn,
the barren strife,
the stone of the alone
blind deaf dumb.
In raptures of participation
all art is born.
Joy wills the world
wills even despair
to be overcome
in the loves of creation.

*

Nikolai, here's the perch of a season suited
for mountaineers and eagles and prophesying poets.
Here on the bough of friendship above the winds
except for some cherub-zephyrs, we've leisure to clap
the wings of our meditation and share a song,
share a silence. Throw down a star or two
out of the clusters knocking against our brows
as a birthday gift for Stalin.
O, the earth
carries more messages than the radios know.
In shivered grass and rubadub under the ribs
our morse breaks all transmissions and suddenly
decoded in any language as music announces
the Earth of Judgment and the Angelic Spring
tapping on every grave for at least a crocus,
a chrism of light to anoint the trysted lovers
under the wreath of the shadow.
But we're old hands

at spring-games. We can relax and watch awhile
old ferments that we helped to brew maturing
in the blunt head of the Atlas-seedling uplifting
a trophy-crumb of soil and the twined fingers
of the young lovers isled in the forest-hush
and the workers united in stark noonlight of liberty
and a world of things a world of loveliest things
manifold Earth and its dogged transformations

and man with work and play
so tangled in the quick of transformations
he cannot sort out which is which.

But first the Earth of Judgment and the Spring
a Michael of trumpets against the city of whores
crying *Woe Woe* that Great City
clothed in fine linen and purple and scarlet.
For its merchants were
the Great Men of the Earth,
for by its sorceries
was all mankind deceived.
For in it is the blood of the Prophets and the Saints,
of all who were martyred on the Earth.

*

After the smoke of its burning seen far off at sea
there will be simply the Earth of the Poets and of Lenin
and on that day this poem will rise up
and go out into the streets
and go out into the meadows
and everyone will be inside this poem
and the poem will be a single meadow flower
trampled by the dancers
and then the poem will be high up in the singing air
and then upon the lips of all the dancers singing.

To Ann

When lovers meet

at deep noon or midnight
the torrent of history
pours roaring on them

When lovers meet
the bleak tides of darkness
cove them seeking
each cranny of weakness

When lovers meet
they meet many friends
all the stars reflected
in a point of dew

When lovers meet
secure in the stormwind
Life hands then all things:
'Redeem, transform.'

When lovers meet
I meet you always
I know in my heart
the love then redeemed

When lovers met
I meet you always
in the breaking hearty
in the depths transformed

When lovers meet
nothing is lost:
the communist future
once grasped in our hands

When loves meet
all bitterness goes
the memory still
of that future is mine.

Where are We Hopelessly Wrong?

written during a committee meeting at Marx House, 1953

The plumes of heat are sprinkling dust
Our faces lift their furtive lids
close down again and bodies creak
upon the chairs of polyp growth

Higher we rise on tenuous stakes
of comprehension till we rub
green-haloed heads along the ceiling
then sink upon a spike of fear

and look again on our own faces
from unsuspected mirrors set
by enemies in midst of words
to turn them on more complex axes

and yet the world is never further
than the revolving windows blown
by the dark breath of weathercocks
into the dawn of all the peoples

In the Night of Warsaw

to Bertolt Brecht also in the Hotel Bristol, 1952

I looked down from the window high above the street
and saw in the opposite ruin a cleared-out space
with an arc light cutting the midnight
and in the heart of the light two dancers
and I thought of you asleep in a room below
and the Warsaw of rubble all round us in the shattered night.
And there was no one alive in Warsaw that moment
in Warsaw in Poland on the earth
but the couple who danced in the jag-edged island of light.
and it didn't seem to matter,
it was possible, necessary, and good,
that no one was left alive but a dancing couple,
as long as they danced in the wound in the rib of night,
as long as they danced.

I who have praised the summer abundance,
the hand-in-hand dancers ringing the earth,
and have said that nothing else justifies our struggle,
I have always felt more at home in winter
in loss privation aloneness
in the absolute of death.

I distrust all easy embraces,
all gifts whatsoever, a words
save those that have passed he test of silence..
we must recognise alienation
before we can live unalienated,
recognise it in our bones and the sudden shaft of light,
the momentary impact
when we are all men because we are nobody,
when we are alive because we are dead,
when we are in contact because we are cut off.
I see you smiling as you talk.
I see the dancers circling the fragile islands of survival.
after all I do not care what happens,
what happens to myself or anyone,
as long as the dancers are there, ignoring us all.

At the heart of my darkness,
at the heart of your silence as you smile.

Where could they dance excerpt in the night of Warsaw?

Randall Swingler at Pebmarsh

The daffodil-stars break gold
in a mist of green and grey,
the grasses prick from the mould,
and the clencht buds unfold
on the apple-branch, grown bold
in the circling whites of day.

Randall stares at the round
of swelling earth, and smiles.
What rhymes may best expound
The tangle and order found
in a rood of English ground
with Spring at her hedgerow-wiles?

O the song goes deep and deep
in the oak-roots of the wood,
in the ploughland's marshalled sweep
there the lads one day will reap
the song with the corn and heap
the barns of brotherhood.

While the new harmonies ring,
break through with plough and pen
where thrush and daffodil bring
the insurrection of Spring
in a challenge echoing
along the hedges of men.

Paris Midnight

to Tristan Tzara at a corner of the Boulevard St Michel

Tristan you first discovered
under bibles, advertisement-hoardings, and metaphysics
that Chaos was not a primordial condition
but an involuntary invention
of bourgeois cuttlefish
exuding darkness to confuse the issue
and find themselves at home

Your lot was harder than that of Herakles:
You had to fight a hydra-world of copulas
with every momentary monster
a lie, an injustice, a selfrighteous murder;
cleanse the dunged stables of our sleep
by propagandising among the winds
and educating dungbeetles to a proper sense
of their historic mission;
penetrate the smug parlours
of patriarchal hell
with all its smell of pisspots and boiled cabbage,
dissociation of sensibility
and stock-exchange ticker-tape
etcetera etcetera
bitter and bitterer
jobs for a poet on a night of spring
with all a million million leaves outbursting
from the joint of this thumb
his kneejoints and his ears
as he takes root in the delighted earth.

Night breaks its chains
and there is space the colour of abandon
still growing larger under the rain's glazed eye
but you who bind the days to flowers
flowers I say O mockery by cursed temporary sojournes
and well I hear you piercing tunnel-cries
slow suffocations among the debris of men
you flick the whip of the insensible laugh
you knot the wreathe of silence
spring opened in the very midmost of the night
difficult thought unwieldy din of density of smoke
and grace that's spinning like a tree of stars
where some live presence shows its double form
and one is winter's and the other one is joy's
O must I pass between the blindly writhing wakes
by the lusty sea's ripe nakedness
covered alone with mists among the songs of fire
how far must I go following you forbidden face
to the world's root

I see you small as a mole in the night of April
sapping a mountain, careless
if the gigantic crags come down on your head
as long as they come down.
Patient as a statue of bearded granite
deep in the night of Egypt:
you hold your poem like a stopwatch in your hand
counting the moment till the hidden fuse explodes
the accumulated tensions of a callous world,
the TNT of tentacled anxieties
hooked in the genitals and the Friday payslip
heaped-up in insurance (verified) details
and the hire-purchase deeds
of a modern-convenient maisonette in hell
Suddenly pity like an explosion of silence
is knocking, knocking
knocking at a door where no door was
knocking at a heart where no heart was

and the door opens, the heart breaks.
The possibility of being human
appears, as the final abstraction opens its desert

Giants of rainstorm summerfreshness
O depths of idle glitterings
still I go trying the most sure defeats
am I not he who from afar sees himself live and die
thus I go turning over leaves of serial landscapes
tearing torn and faithful
deadwood flesh and earth
ill-chosen persevering
from one halt to the next

I am horse I am river

I get along badly all the same I live

But after the last copula of lie and law
of cruelty and duality
is broken, there remains
the counter-task of the sevenday fiats
a universe to be recreated
clean up from bedrock every moment
shamelessly caught in a reckless flashlight
man emerging from nether forests
with eyes bewildered, the convalescence
painful after the night of knives
the anguish of learning a new language
where money won't modify every incidence
of grammar and meaning
the rediscovery of flint and grass
mountain-spring and depths of ocean
the moon in the woman's opening belly
the sun of righteousness in the man's breast
the terrible moment of truth
when every mirror on earth lies shattered
by the pressure within of cruel images

and men must look in each other's eyes
for verification of existence
an endless journey on hardship's ridges
and an immediate goal
recognized with the bowels' lucidity,
all this and more you needed to order
here in the Paris of alienation

what do I lack untended forces
of light's enchantments
I grafted fragile life
on vigorous laughter of mountains
where old memories of rubble wastelands
are slumbering in my flesh
listen immensity outside
is breaking in the trees
the fruit of castanets
is lighted up in the cascade
you waken the sealed fire
in the deceitful dawn
here are winds petrified
in gowns of sleeping women

O stones dance through the night of obdurate ages
numbers and their prey grown visible here below
until you burst into blood's laughter
that earth may now come home on earth
and all its kingdom's seed be multiplied

Let earth at last come home on earth

Christmas Eve 1952

A baby is crying in the wintry world
that closes all its covetous doors.
In the dark manger of the breathing beasts
the outcasts huddle on bare floors.

And still the new life cries in darkness, still
the masters hoard their sweated pence,
and then the abject terrors strike again
to massacre the innocents.

The dawn moves every westward, flowing past
the lines of the dividing maps.
It slides through every window of man, and wakes
the heart upon whose pane it taps.

In vain are bolts and bars against this light,
the cry of life renewed
breaks the old stones, and men uniting stand
against all Herod's brood.

To Ilya Ehrenburg

on his 60th Birthday

The grey clouds race and rumble,
the stormwind tramples by,
the cloud-rack blackens out
the moon from the sky.
But in each gap of the storm
serene she reappears
and a flood of silver transforms
the landscape of fears.

Ilya, you man of tempest,
a whip of truth you crack
to tame the beasts of the thunder
and scare them back;
but when the hush of the moon
spreads out again below,
on the crystals of grey iron
soft petals glow.

Yours is the tenderness strong
when the hour of choice is stark,
to guard the new life crying
in the wild dark.

Yours is the strength tender
amid the throes of that birth,
to fight more fiercely delighting
in the sweetness of earth.

Last Words with Dylan Thomas

So they got you at last despite your guiles of surrender
despite your sleight-of-hand with the apple-of-eden
despite your efforts to carry a piece of darkness
round on the palm of your hand

You walked a tight-rope even on terra firma
you walked the earth even on a tight-rope
you wore the mask of an intricate innocence

And now the people whom you most despised
write lies of praise about you

There was nothing in the world you hated but cruelty
and you loved almost everyone except the people who now praise you
Dylan walking in the midnight of a London
without the penny of a drink in our pocket
you assumed the mask of innocence over you innocence
and affronted the patronising world with a beggar's palm

You were a Robin Hood of tavern thickets
talking through a burnt-our cigarette
taking from the rich to give to the poor,
yourself the poorest
and dodging behind the wildwood of a baffling image

You wept in the cinema at people weeping
you wept and signed the Rosenberg Petition
you frowned and forgot to reach for another drink

You looked out over the cells of fascism and wrote
Light breaks where no sun shines
You looked out on Chamberlain from your hut of indignation and wrote
The hand that signed the paper felled a people
You denounced the guilty men of Nuremberg
in words heavy as clencht fists

But life was a sudden wind from that vats of cider
the distance where a girl dreamed in the
cloverfield of her body
and grief was the lair of thunder in the oceanic shell
you smiled and reached for another pot of beer

You looked out from your bitter eyes of innocence
and knew it all and hid in your gentleness

We shall not walk again the London of a midnight

You knew it all, the map of our sharp-edged conflicts
and hoarsely whispered your indignant pity

I am for the people
I am against all who are against the people

But the map's contours blurred in your angry tear
in the wheeling iris-lights of the lovely earth
you smiled and reached out for another beer

And life was a lifted wave with the naked image
borne on the curved shell of the mastered elements
the snakes of the wind in the tresses of blown gold
and the mouth of a sudden kiss come close and closest

I am for life
I am against all who are against life

You turned back to the childhood of a hayhigh sweetness
and climbed the stairs of water
seeking a thousand ways through the walls of murder
that closed the streets of daily life about you
into the endless spiral of the rose-heart

But because your face was innocent under a guileful mask
of innocence
you always came on people
the dark tunnel of silence led to the friendly voices
the vortex of blind growth came still to rest
on the familiar faces of common people
worn by life as stones are worn by water
and you loved them even more than you loved the stones
the delicate maze of the revolving rose
broke into the clear face of your wife
and you were home again
in the daily streets yet closed with the walls of murder
seeking another way to break and pierce them
the way of simple union and shared needs
the lionheart of honey the furious tooth of salt
the spinning wheel of the cottage-flower
the children's voices kiteflown in the dusk
the body of labour broken as bread is broken
and given in daily renewal
the lap of sleep and the ultimate round of dancing
But they got you at last before you had clambered through
they caught you halfway in the hole you had made in the walls,
scraping at midnight, hiding the mortar in pockets
they caught you helpless they broke you across the back
and broke you across the brow
and you smiled in your sleep

So near you had come. The flowers of endless gardens
not yet sown from the wayward aprons of wind
sent their warm lights upon you and you smiled

The murderers got you Dylan
and now they praise you in their church of death
and those who were waiting with outstretched hands to drag you
up the jagged shores of safety
mourn and remember you another way.

We turned to look at the dawn gone out of your eyes
and burning securely along the shores of the gathering peoples
and there your play with the apple has lost the sting of its guile.

Sudden Discords in the Trumpets of Overdelayed Last Judgment, 1956

We were looking another way
when the bomb blew up the bridge,
blew up all bridges, it seemed.
We stood in abject dismay
on an island of devastation.
All familiar shapes were dimmed,
twisted. In consternation
we took out our maps, but the roads
had changed their names and directions.
The imposing landmarks were gone.

For a while we wandered on,
with no one to answer our questions.
Our calls had no echoes. At last
we halted in huddling fear
as winds from all quarters blustered.

In the endless night I dreamed
that my own Face came near
from the other end of space.
grinning, unscarred, ungrieving.
'You knew it all,' my voice said,
'I'm the one you'll never deceive.
Don't lie any more or you're damned
to the dingiest ditches of hell.'

'I knew nothing,' I weakly replied.
I knew nothing. And yet you knew,
you blandly assert. You could tell
the insidious lies from the true.'

My otherself said with a sneer,
'Dialectical insight you claimed,
but never once grasped, it's quite clear,
the deep nature of contradictions,
the darkness, the guile there, as well
as the obvious opposites clashing.
Only a child could believe
that life with loud cheers would advance
on such a straightforward track.
Laired in paradise regained
is the subtly satanic curse.'

'I'm lost, I've no compass, no guide.'
'Then there's some hope. You must pierce
to the core of the moving whole
with it's tangle of choice and of chance,
its shrouded and shining goal.
Now cast all illusions aside,
but reject disillusionment too.'

I woke in the sudden morning
with stormclouds luridly spread.
The road was there, baffled and torn,
glimpsed and then brokenly lost,
with all ditches and dangers crisscrossed
in its zigzag towards the unknown.

Yet I saw how it led on ahead.
I saw there was no turning-back.
I was one of a host, and alone.
Alone, I was one of a host.

At the Heart of the Maze of Fetishes

to Edith Sitwell in London, at the Sesame Club, after lunch

In Trafalgar Square, the heart of the maze of fetishes,
the mask of the snake sodden with black blood,
the ragged knife of stone and the idol blotcht with nail-heads:

along the Embankment the naked women wailing
with rivermud bubbling in the wounds of their faces
and the sacred harlots sprawled in the streets of Westminster:

who does not see these things is blind with the single sight
that reflects dead surfaces only. The midnight worships
spiked in the mangrove-swamps migrate at a crueller magic,
commodity-fetishism; and Europe, with all it's complex history
sunk to a radio-whine of pretences and abstract skills,
leaves Africa human, itself a mere market of deathdolls.

The faces in London streets are stranger to me than masks of the Congo.
The terror is there, and the menace, but flabby with daydream evasion.
The terror is there, nut blurred and evaded, shapeless.

The masterful planes intersecting – the power over space.
The ripening rhythms of dance – the power over time.
These are gone. All are gone. But the terror remains.

The Thing remains. The Thing with power over all.
We are lost in the maze of the fetishes, things of the Thing.
And he who can't see it has had all his eyes pickt way
by vultures of money in deserts of lonely sleep.

And yet
when the façade leans out, cricks, cracks with a puff of dust
we see the hidden faces that crawl beneath our wallpapers
and melt with medusa-chills on the clammy pillow of tears.

Then is the moment to walk through the wall of granite.
The doorway is suddenly there. The light of the future
comes beating up from behind the high red ramparts of longing.

The poet catches in a single palm
the lice brusht out of the fur of the sliddering devil
and the lichens of crystal blown from the world far ahead.

The exposed present is the cross of love
and the wings of transfiguration, amoeba-division
and a body of light that leaps from the furthest horizon.

And something else, that unites and divides, in judgement;
in action, divides and unites:

and so
you hold in your open hand
the forest of ancient sleep
with a moon in every pool
and fernsides grottoed deep.

In a frock of sprigged muslin
a naiad informs each shadow
and a dance-ring burns silver
turning in each meadow.

There in the spiralling silence
the smith in his cave of smoke
beats iron for all men
and knots for the stormy oak.

This moment is your pulse
when the façade falls down
and the deathless girl of the kiss
is every girl in town.

When poetry comes true
and England at last uprises
the song then meets at each turn of the streets
its own wildwood surprises.

The mirrow of transformations
cracks in its jealous flame
as men and women each moment
beat it at its own game.

New dares, new tests and trials
confront the poet then –
without a Bethlehem strawcrown
among his fellowmen.

For he who watched the murder
must sham that he's not there
or that he's out of his legal wits
with straw in his penniless hair.

Meanwhile you hold in your hand
the jagging lights of hell,
the thicket of ancient sleep,
and the dream, the saving spell.

The Perspective for Art

to my niece Cressida

The faceless ogres grow so daily
we scarcely note their speedway shadow
scorch the grass across the meadow,
the hellstreets paved with good intentions,
the houses ghostly as a tombstone.
The announcer coughs but never mentions
the ubiquitous tick of dryrot doom
consuming slowly
estranging wholly.

The bloated city blurts with smoke,
the agued country's raked with damp.
The eunuch furies leave their stamp
on all, till our policed desires,
batoned around the close of can't,
feel freely only when gangster fires
from film-pools of narcistic phantoms.
We yawn, unwoken;
still the dogmatic slumber's unbroken.

The Good Life – where's a just directive?
Truth, naked as a rose is red,
without a pistol at her head;
Man mated with the Universe
in a fourposted depthless bed,
shedding the headlong birthborn curse
and signing amnesties with the dead.
The dream gives art a full perspective,
and nothing else, when all is said.

Song of a Refugee from the Twenties

to Edgell Rickword, in the later 1960's, at Halstead

When we were young we also knocked
on obsolete doors with unanswered knocks.
No one was ever so young we thought.
Our time is ticking in no clocks.

The young are always right
even when they are wrong.
I thought so then and I think so still.
Truth's only speech is a song.

But we were a mere handful
scruffy in odd corners of beer.
No one noticed us except
for an unimportant sneer.

Then a few years ago,
an old man in a London street,
I roused myself from an abstract thought
and nobody to meet,

and all around me I saw
the girls with wildwood hair
and the lads with ridiculous beards:
all our dead friends were there

suddenly all-sides multiplied.
The small daft bunch was a host,
and myself in my resurrected youth
a dumb irrelevant ghost.

Three Family Poems

1   To My Brother Ray

Memory is a curious country
with many a wellplanned street,
then tricky bogs and murky traps
on every side are met.
Years sink in a dull confusion,
but on day stands complete

for no particular reason
which we can well descry
save that a girl turns gaily,
a cloud swags in the sky,
and a hush sweeps across the earth
or an inexplicable cry.

The limelight of dead passions
on the dismantled stage
produces odd effects at times,
moving our mirth or rage.
We clap or want our money back,
call the author fool or sage.

And that indeed we should expect
with every actor a ghost,
the prompter longdead in his box
and all the stage-sets lost,
no clocks at all left in the world
and Time laid to our cost.

Come enter the pit a moment.
I wonder can you tell
that face which weeps, that face which smiles,
that face exposed for sale,
that face which glitters and goes out
or wears a mask so well.

2 To My Brother Philip

Out of this earth we were born.
Without your eyes to read,
Your tongue to answer back,
the words are thin and lack
the resonance of your scorn,
your huge enjoyment. I need
your reassurance here
out of our difficult youth
to tell me if I am near
or far from the brotherly truth.

A poet, at the hasty start,
may be arrogant enough
to want no ears for his call,
or nothing less than all.
And yet with a change of heart
in the experience of love,
may learn, when the song's been sung,
that he wants no more at the end
than one or two called friend
who speak the same mother-tongue.

3 To My Father Norman Alone in the Blue Mountains

Though you in your hermitage
of cold and scornful stone,
of tranquil and ruthless light,
refuse to accept these pages,
what other name can I write
over the arch of the ruin
made my sole monument?
Your rejecting word I ignore
and call up your name once more,
though you will pay no heed
though you will never read
these words in your mountain-lair.

So long for you alone
I wrote, all my thoughts I bent
on you as friend and foe
so long, no name I know
but yours for this empty space
now Ray and Phil are both gone
and the spiralling fury of Time
bores remorselessly on.

As a bitter tribute then take
these pages that strip me bare
in death's thin bleakening ray.
Turn for a moment I say
turn from your obdurate place
in that clarity of stone,
that terrible folly of light,
turn for a moment this way
your abstracted face.

In the Wild Surf

to my daughter Helen, on the beach at St Ives, Cornwall

The billow arches and turns
in a cavern of tumbling gold.
Arch your young back and ride,
gaily trustful and bold,
the curve of the elements
in a shared strength and pride.

There by the greendark rocks,
as the tide ebbs out, there swings
the undertow ever more near.

How warn you of cruel things
when the heart needs confidence?
must I sow suspicion and fear?

I see your uplifted face
in the hurrying light of the wave.
Akin to the wildness you go:
that's the one comfort I find.
I can do nothing to save,
counsel, or tell what I know.

Out of one depth curls the wave,
from another you rise up clear
and meet the bright dangerous day.
Cut off on the barren sand,
I can only love you from here
where the wind blows my words away.

On Nuclear Physics and
The Resolving Truth Beyond It

to my son Philip

How take the world to pieces, then
put it alive together again?
The problem's crashed upon us all
since Humpty Dumpty had his fall
crackt from the bumptious abstract wall –
since consciousness of human fate
made us feel direly separate
yet merged with something far more great,
our lives a fragmentary part,
yet pulses of a single heart.

Only in momentary vision
the trick's been done, the bits defined
in analytic lockt precision
inside the seamless unity
both ultimate and immediate
with ceaseless changes, fiery, free,
which form the stable stormy whole.

But now the breaking point is near
and we must use our better wits,
not merely count more bits and bits
in treacherous ghost-infinities,
a world where nothing human fits.

Yes, we must choose the harder goal
and grasp the method that will bind
both vision and analysis
in steady focus, till we see
the quarrelling aspects one,
the leap
into new wholes, the structures struck
from the extending symmetries
where number breeds and plays its role
ever more complex in division,
but under unity's clear control.
No need for atomising fear.
Courage will give us back our luck.

There is no forward way but this.

Remembering Robert Kett

To Meta

Still earth is there. Even though windows close,
the wind hangs sprawling in the apple-boughs.
Now Autumn thuds with falls, the hedges thin,
and the winged seeds go sweeping by or spin.
Beet-clumps are grey beside the plaited rick,
The chimney-starling gives his chuckling click.
Spring will come stumbling back, no doubt it's true;
the Seasons turning in a globe of dew,
the unborn Spring, within us deep we know.
My heart is dead four hundred years ago.

Life is enough. The heart with sweetness breaks
and all a dusk of nightingales awakes.
For beauty's hush is laired in memory's shell
and the whorled past from which our musicks swell
is cavernous with death. All roses start
our of the dark where burns a dead girl's heart.
I am awakened by the dreaming dead
and dare not ask who shares my tumbled bed;
to murdered lovers all my joys I owe.
My heart's alive four hundred years ago.

Life is enough and gold the Earth remains,
beyond our depths, in all her spendthrift grains.
Death is Life's heart-of-hearts. The pulse that drives
breaks as it stores: one death is various lives.
Rich with its roots entwined among the dead
the red rose salves the wood from which it's bred.
O Love, the little sun stoops at our will
and out of songs the Earth awakens still;
yet here my living heart, in Silence, hears
my buried heart that holds four hundred years.

The Fetish Thing

Marx struggled all his days to free
our minds and hearts from slavish lies,
so we might live in harmony
with nature and our fellows here.
Look round and what a world we see.
Each day more mad divisions rise
out of that blinding hate and fear
deep-rooted in the Fetish Thing.

And what if we who boast his name
in our resistance, soon or late
harden and find the truth become
a closed-in system, a mere sum
of this and that, and flatly succumb
to the arithmetic of fissioning hell:
truth that should be a reckless flame
to burn and break all barriers built
between us and the sacred spring
of life upbubbling in ceaseless change.

Whose then is the greater guilt?

Yes, how displace the men of hate,
the men of fear, if we as well
lose the quick secret, spoil the spell
that links us with the unlivening whole,
so that, estranged, we cease to range
the hills of hope, the heights of vision,
the depths of struggle, and grasp no more
the suddenly naked human core,
its terrible and exalting force.

Come turn away
into the full involving day,
accept the piercing interplay
of opposites, accept at last
the way that stormtosst life holds fast
its clear and unpredictable course,
its lost and ever-present goal.

It Has Happened

to Patricia Moberley

It has happened all before, and yet
it has all to happen. So it seems.
Darker grows the maniac threat
and richer swell the answering dreams.
Just past our straining fingertips
it lies. And that's the very thing
they said two thousand years ago,
broken, with hope unslackening.
At every gain, away it slips.
In struggle, entire and strong it grows;
the bonds of brotherhood hold fast.
Someday the treacherous gap will close
and we'll possess the earth at last.

Notes

Summering Song
Robert Kett was one of the leaders of peasant protests against the enclosure of common land in Norfolk in 1549. 'Captain Pouch' was the leader of a peasant rising against the enclosure of common land in Leicestershire and Warwickshire in the early 1600s. Both men were eventually captured and hanged. This poem was published as 'Voice of the Wheat' in *New Lyrical Ballads* (edited with Maurice Carpenter and Honor Arundel 1945).

Who Are the English?
John Ball was a Lollard priest who took a prominent part in the Peasants' Revolt of 1331. Jack Cade was the leader of a peasant rebellion in Kent in 1450. John Wycliffe (1320-1384) was a theologian who advocated the translation of the Bible into English; his followers were known as Lollards.

Christmas Eve 1937
Ernst Thälmann (1886-1944) was the leader of the German Communist Party during the Weimar Republic. He was arrested in 1933 and held in solitary confinement for eleven years. He was murdered in Buchenwald in 1944. Tom Mooney (1882-1942) was a trade-union activist, sentenced to life imprisonment for alleged involvement in the in 1916 Preparedness Day bombing in San Francisco. As a result of an international campaign to secure his release, he was eventually pardoned in 1939. Uriah Butler (1897-1977) was a trade-union leader in Trinidad and Tobago, imprisoned in 1937 by the colonial authorities for organizing industrial action in the oilfields. Luis Prestes (1898-1990) was one of the leaders of the Brazilian Populoar Front, imprisoned in 1935 by the Vargas dictatorship. The Communist miners' leader Mick Kane was imprisoned in 1936 for organising a six-month strike for union recognition at Harworth colliery in Nottinghamshire. George Chandler, John Smith and William Carney were also miners who were imprisoned during the Harworth dispute.

On Guard for Spain

On Guard for Spain was first published in *Left Review* in March 1937, then published as a 1d pamphlet. It was staged as a Mass Declamation at Unity Theatre in April 1937 and subsequently all over the UK to raise money for Medical Aid for Spain.

Requiem Mass for Englishmen Fallen in the International Brigade

Ralph Fox, John Cornford, Wilf Jobling, Moishe Davidovich, Jack Atkinson, James Wark, Bill Briskey, Alan Craig, Robert Symes, Tommy Dolan, T.J. Carter and Sid Avner were all members of the British Communist Party who died fighting in Spain with the International Brigades.

Peace is our Answer

This sequence was published in 1950 in a book of the same name, together with poems by Paul Éluard, Louis Aragon and Pablo Neruda and linocuts by Noel Counihan.

Peace Has 400,000,000 Names

In 1950 the World Peace Council launched the Stockholm Appeal, calling for an absolute ban on nuclear weapons. Lindsay was on the committee of the Stockholm World Authors Peace Appeal, attending the 1948 World Congress of Intellectuals for Peace in Wroclaw and the 1949 Paris Peace Congress. Notable signatories included Louis Aragon, Thomas Mann, Pablo Picasso and Dimitri Shostakovich.

Cry of Greece: A Mass Declamation

Originally published in 1950 by Arena with a woodcut by Gerald Marks as a 3d broadsheet to raise money for the League of Democracy in Greece.

Buffalo Stadium, Paris, 1948

Paul Éluard (1895-1952), was a French poet, one of the founders of the Surrealist movement, later a member of the French Communist Party. He was a member of the Congress of Intellectuals for Peace.

Pablo Neruda at Stalingrad, 1949
Pablo Neruda (1904-1973) was a Chilean Communist poet and diplomat and winner of the 1971 Nobel Prize for Literature. He was a signatory to the Stockholm Appeal.

Nikolai Tikhonov
Nikolai Tikhonov (1896-1979) was a Georgian-born poet and chair of the Soviet Writers Union (dismissed for being too close to Zoschenko and Ahmatova). He was also the first chair of the Soviet Peace Committee.

To Ann
Ann Davies (1914-54) was a Unity Theatre actress and the manager of Fore Publications. She and Lindsay lived together from 1944 until her death.

In the Night of Warsaw
Bertolt Brecht (1898-1956) was a German poet, playwright and theatre director, best known for plays like *Drums in the Night, The Threepenny Opera, Fear and Misery in the Third Reich, Mother Courage and Her Children* and *The Caucasian Chalk Circle.*

Randall Swingler at Pebmarsh
Randall Swingler (1909-67) was a Communist poet and novelist. He edited *Left Review, Our Time* and (with Lindsay) *Arena.* Swingler and Lindsay were directors of Fore Publications, which published *Three Letters to Nikolai Tikhonov.* The Swinglers lived in Pebmarsh, not far from the Lindsays' home in Castle Hedingham.

Paris Midnight
Tristan Tzara (1896-1963) was a Romanian and French poet and essayist and one of the founders of the Dada movement. Lindsay wrote about his relationship with Tzara in *Meetings with Poets* (1968).

To Ilya Ehrenburg
Ilya Ehrenburg (1891-1967) was a Soviet poet and novelist, best known for *The Thaw, The Fall of Paris* and *The Black Book* (edited with Vassily Grossman). He was a war-correspondent during the First and Second World Wars and the Spanish Civil War. He was a signatory to the Stockholm Appeal.

Last Words with Dylan Thomas
Dylan Thomas (1914-1953) was a poet, best known for *Deaths and Entrances, A Child's Christmas in Wales* and *Under Milk Wood*. Lindsay wrote about his relationship with Thomas in *Meetings with Poets*.

Sudden Discords in the Trumpets of Overdelayed Last Judgment, 1956
At the 20th Congress of the Soviet Communist Party in February 1956, the new Soviet leadership attacked the 'cult of personality' and revealed the extent of the Stalin tyranny. In November Soviet troops re-entered Budapest to prevent Hungary leaving the Warsaw Pact. By the end of the year over 7,000 members (a fifth of the entire membership) had left the British Communist Party, including many of Lindsay's closest friends.

At the Heart of the Maze of Fetishes
Edith Sitwell (1887-1964) was a poet and critic, best known for her collections *Gold Coast Customs, The Song of the Cold* and *Façade* (set to music by William Walton). Lindsay published her *The Shadow of Cain* at Fore Publications. He wrote about their relationship in *Meetings with Poets* and in an unpublished MS 'The Starfish Road'.

The Perspective for Art
Cressida Lindsay (1930-2010) was a novelist and the daughter of Lindsay's younger brother Philip.

Song of a Refugee from the Twenties
Edgell Rickword (1898-1982) was a Communist poet and critic. He edited the *Calendar of Modern Letters, Left Review*, and *Our Time*, and with Lindsay the anthology *A Handbook of Freedom*. In 1958 he moved to Halstead in Essex, not far from the Lindsays' home in Castle Hedingham.

Three Family Poems
Ray Lindsay (1903-1960) was a distinguished painter and book-illustrator. Philip Lindsay (1906–1958) wrote many books of historical fiction and biography. He was one of the writers responsible for Paul Robeson's *Song of Freedom*. Norman Lindsay (1879-1969) was one of the most important Australian painters of the twentieth-century.